南京市公共服务领域英文译写指南

Guidelines for English Translations in Public Service Areas in Nanjing

南京市人民政府外事办公室　主编

南京出版传媒集团
南京出版社

图书在版编目（CIP）数据

南京市公共服务领域英文译写指南 / 南京市人民政府外事办公室主编. -- 南京：南京出版社, 2025.1

ISBN 978-7-5533-4594-9

Ⅰ. ①南… Ⅱ. ①南… Ⅲ. ①公共服务－英语－翻译－南京－指南②公共服务－英语－写作－南京－指南 Ⅳ. ①C916.2-62

中国国家版本馆CIP数据核字（2024）第027922号

书　　名　南京市公共服务领域英文译写指南
主　　编　南京市人民政府外事办公室
执　　行　江苏舜禹国际语言服务出口基地
出版发行　南京出版传媒集团
　　　　　　南 京 出 版 社
社　　址　南京市玄武区太平门街53号
邮　　编　210016
联系电话　025-83283873、83283864（营销）　025-83112257（编务）

策划统筹　包敬静
责任编辑　包敬静　邹云香
装帧设计　石　慧
责任印制　杨福彬

排　　版　南京新华丰制版有限公司
印　　刷　南京爱德印刷有限公司
开　　本　880毫米×1230毫米　1/32
印　　张　10.25
字　　数　156千
版　　次　2025年1月第1版
印　　次　2025年6月第2次印刷
书　　号　ISBN 978-7-5533-4594-9
定　　价　68.00元

编委会

序　言

规范公共服务领域的英文译写，提升语言环境治理水平，有助于消除文化误解，促进文化交流互鉴，是城市国际化程度和国家文明文化的象征。作为外籍人士获取城市信息的重要载体和展示城市文化的直观名片，公共领域外文标识不仅关系到外籍人士的生活便利，更直接影响到城市的国际形象和吸引力。但由于涉外标识点多、面广、量大，设置主体多元且专业性强、缺乏统一的参照标准，仍存在语义失准现象。

2023 年，南京市人民政府外事办公室牵头组建由高校教授、外籍专家和省市外事翻译中心组成的专家组，在各有关单位支持下，经多次专家评审会论证，历时两年完成这本《南京市公共服务领域英文译写指南》（简称《指南》）。

为确保准确性和实用性，我们参考了2017版国家标准《公共服务领域英文译写规范》、2009版江苏省地方标准《公共场所标识英文译写规范》及国际通用译写规范开展细致的编译，对过时或错误的译法进行了调整优化，增加了符合当代发展语境的新词汇。《指南》共分九部分，分别是通则、道路交通、商业服务、文化旅游、教育体育、医疗卫生、政务服务、组织机构和南京特色词汇，共3000多词条。每一部分都统一了译写规范，详细解读了该部分英文译写的总体要求、具体译法和书写标准。通则在实际应用中具有重要的指导作用，能够帮助我们更加准确地开展英文译写。《指南》收录的反映南京地方文化特色词汇涉及本地的历史遗址、旅游景区和衣食住行。

使用《指南》有助于避免翻译歧义，减少因语言障碍导致的误解和困惑，让大家在翻译上更方便，也让外国友人在出行、饮食、就医等方面获得更加便捷的体验。我们希望通过《指南》的出版，更加系统、全面地提升南京市公共服务领域英文译写的水平，推进实现出入境、投资贸易和生活的便利化，持续打造国际一流营商环境。

《指南》是各位编委专家智慧的结晶，在此谨向王守仁、丁言仁两位教授以及为编写付出辛勤努力的全体同仁表示最诚挚的谢意！感谢江苏舜禹国家语言服务出口基地和南京出版社在出版过程中提供的服务保障！

南京市人民政府外事办公室

2024年12月

目　录

Contents

一、通则

1. 设施及服务信息 …………………………………… 11
2. 通用警示警告信息 ………………………………… 23
3. 通用指示说明信息 ………………………………… 30
4. 消防安全提示信息 ………………………………… 35

二、道路交通

1. 道路交通设施信息 ………………………………… 45
2. 交通运输服务信息 ………………………………… 51
(1) 航空客运 …………………………………… 51
(2) 铁路客运 …………………………………… 55
(3) 轮船客运 …………………………………… 58
(4) 轨道交通客运 ……………………………… 59
(5) 公共汽车客运 ……………………………… 59
(6) 出租车客运 ………………………………… 61
(7) 通用类 ……………………………………… 62

3. 交通警示指示说明信息 …… 69
4. 南京市重要交通枢纽 …… 77

三、商业服务

1. 商业场所及服务信息 …… 85
（1）商业场所和机构名称 …… 85
（2）商业设施及服务项目名称 …… 89
（3）商品种类名称 …… 91
（4）商业部门名称 …… 101
（5）商业从业人员名称 …… 102
2. 餐饮业场所及服务信息 …… 105
（1）餐饮业场所和机构名称 …… 105
（2）菜单及中西菜肴名称 …… 106
（3）酒水名称 …… 114
（4）调味品名称 …… 116
（5）餐具名称 …… 117
（4）餐饮业从业人员名称 …… 119
3. 酒店业场所及服务信息 …… 120
（1）酒店业场所名称 …… 120
（2）酒店业用品及设施名称 …… 124
（3）酒店业从业人员名称 …… 126

4. 金融业场所及服务信息 …… 127
（1）金融业场所和机构名称 …… 127
（2）金融业设施名称 …… 129
（3）金融业从业人员名称 …… 130
5. 商业服务信息提示 …… 131
（1）餐饮业 …… 131
（2）酒店业 …… 133
（3）金融业 …… 134
（4）通用类 …… 137
6. 新经济领域 …… 139

四、文化旅游

1. 文化场馆名称 …… 148
2. 文化场馆设施及服务信息 …… 151
3. 旅游设施及服务信息 …… 154
4. 文化旅游纪念品 …… 160
5. 其他文化相关信息 …… 163
（1）节假日名称 …… 163
（2）传统文化领域 …… 165
6. 文旅警示指示说明信息 …… 170

五、教育体育

1. 教育领域公共场所及服务信息 …… 180
2. 高校内设机构名称 …… 189
3. 中小学及幼儿园内设机构名称 …… 190
4. 教育系统人员名称 …… 192
5. 驻宁高校名称 …… 193
6. 南京市属学校名称 …… 195
7. 体育场馆名称 …… 196
8. 体育运动项目名称 …… 199
9. 体育场馆设施名称 …… 203
10. 南京市体育场馆名称 …… 206

六、医疗卫生

1. 医疗卫生机构名称 …… 213
2. 医院功能设施及名称 …… 217
3. 医院科室名称 …… 225
4. 检查化验项目名称 …… 230
5. 医疗措施名称 …… 233
6. 医学保障设施名称 …… 236
7. 南京市医疗卫生机构名称 …… 237
8. 医疗警示指示说明信息 …… 241

七、政务服务

1. 政务服务机构名称 …… 249
2. 政务服务业务名称 …… 251
3. 政务服务窗口名称 …… 255

八、组织机构、职务职称

1. 南京市市级组织机构名称 …… 267
（1）中共南京市委相关组织机构名称 ……267
（2）南京市人大相关组织机构名称 ……268
（3）南京市政府相关组织机构名称 ……270
（4）南京市政协相关组织机构名称 ……272
（5）南京市法院、检察院、海关相关组织机构名称 ……273
（6）南京市群众团体相关组织机构名称 ……274
（7）南京市政府派出机构 ……275
（8）南京市其他组织机构名称 ……275
2. 南京市区级组织机构名称 …… 276
（1）南京市辖区名称 ……276
（2）区级党委及群团相关组织机构名称 ……277
（3）区人大相关组织机构名称 ……278
（4）区政府相关组织机构名称 ……279
（5）区政协相关组织机构名称 ……282

（6）区级法院、检察院组织机构名称 ……283
3. 南京市市级相关职务通用名称 ……283
（1）中共南京市委职务通用名称 ……283
（2）南京市人大常委会职务通用名称 ……284
（3）南京市政府职务通用名称 ……285
（4）南京市政协职务通用名称 ……285
（5）南京市中级人民法院职务通用名称 ……286
（6）南京市人民检察院职务通用名称 ……286
（7）南京市级机关部、委、办、局职务通用名称 ……287
4. 南京市区级相关职务通用名称 ……288
（1）区委职务通用名称 ……288
（2）区人大常委会职务通用名称 ……289
（3）区政府职务通用名称 ……289
（4）区政协职务通用名称 ……290
（5）区级委、办、局职务通用名称 ……290
5. 综合管理类公务员职级名称 ……291

九、南京特色词汇

1. 城市名片 ……297
2. 产业发展 ……300
（1）指导产业 ……300
（2）科创园区 ……302

3. 南京市旅游景区 …………………………………………………… 303
4. 南京市文博场馆 …………………………………………………… 306
5. 南京美食 ……………………………………………………………… 308

一、通　则

Part 1 General rules

1. 范围

本部分规定了南京市公共服务领域英文译写的相关术语和定义、译写原则、译写要求和方法、书写要求等。

本部分适用于南京市公共服务领域各类设施及功能、警示和提示等公共服务信息的英文译写。

2. 规范性引用文件

应用本部分内容需参考如下文件。如文件注明日期，则仅注日期的版本适用于本文件。如文件未注日期，则其最新版本（包括所有的修改单）适用于本部分。

中华人民共和国国家通用语言文字法（2000 年 10 月 31 日第九届全国人民代表大会常务委员会第十八次会议通过）

汉语拼音方案（1958 年中华人民共和国第一届全国人民代表大会第五次会议审议通过）

GB 17733 地名 标志

GB/T 10001（所有部分）标志用公共信息图形符号

GB/T 16159 汉语拼音正词法基本规则

GB/T 30240.1—2013 公共服务领域英文译写规范（第 1 部分：通则）

DB32/T 1446.1—2009 公共场所英文译写规范（第 1 部分：通则）

3. 术语和定义

下列术语和定义适用于本部分。

3.1　专名 specific terms

场所和机构名称中用于与同类别、同属性的其他场所或机构相区别，具有唯一性特征的部分。

3.2　通名 generic terms

场所和机构名称中标示场所或机构的类别和属性，不具有唯一性特征的部分。

3.3　场所和机构名称 names of public places and institutions

公共服务领域中具有对外服务功能的公共场所、经营机构、管理机构、企事业单位等。

3.4　设施及功能信息 information of facilities and functions

为满足人们在公共场所活动需要所提供的基础设施、保障设施和服务设施的名称标示及功能指示信息。

3.5　公共服务信息 public service information

为满足人们活动需要，在公共服务领域中提供的功能设施、警示警告、限令禁止、指示指令和说明提示等服务信息。

4. 译写原则

公共场所的英文译写遵从 GB/T 30240《公共服务领域英文译写规范》所规定的合法性原则、规范性原则、服务性原则和文明性原则。

5. 译写要求和方法

5.1 场所和机构名称

5.1.1 总则

场所和机构名称应区分专名、通名、修饰或限定成分，分别使用汉语拼音和英文进行拼写或翻译。

5.1.2 专名

5.1.2.1 专名一般使用汉语拼音拼写，如：“玄武湖” Xuanwu Lake，“玄武”用拼音。

5.1.2.2 来源于英文的专名，直接使用原文，如：“南京奥林匹克体育中心” Nanjing Olympic Sports Center。

5.1.2.3 有实际含义、并需要向服务对象特别说明其含义的专名，可使用英文翻译，如：“侵华日军南京大屠杀遇难同胞纪念馆” The Memorial Hall of the Victims of the Nanjing Massacre by Japanese Invaders。

5.1.3 通名

5.1.3.1 通名一般使用英文翻译，如：“南京大学” Nanjing University，“大学”用英文译出。

5.1.3.2 专名是单音节时，其通名部分可视作专名的一部分，先与专名一起用汉语拼音拼写，然后用英文重复翻译，如：“钟山” Zhongshan Mountain。

5.1.3.3 通名在原文中省略的，应视情况补译，如：“马祥兴”（饭店名）Maxiangxing Restaurant。

5.1.4 修饰或限定成分

5.1.4.1 方位词

方位词包括东、南、西、北、前、后、中、上、内、外，其对应的英文译法分别为 East (E)、South (S)、West (W)、North (N)、Front、Back、Middle、Upper、Inner、

Outer；东南、西南、东北、西北对应的英文译法分别为 Southeast、Southwest、Northeast、Northwest。

5.1.4.2 序数词

通常情况下，其英文写法可采用“No.+ 数字”的形式，如：“南京市第九中学”Nanjing No. 9 Middle School。

5.1.4.3 名从主人情况

现用英文译名已约定俗成的，可根据“名从主人”的原则沿用其习惯的译写方法，如：“中山陵园”Dr. Sun Yat-sen's Mausoleum。

5.2 公共服务信息

5.2.1 总则

公共服务信息使用英文译写。

5.2.2 功能设施信息

5.2.2.1 由设施名称和功能信息两部分组成的语句，应以译出设施的功能信息为主。如：“行李安检通道”Baggage Check，“行李安检”的功能必须译出，“通道”作为设施名称可不必译出。

5.2.2.2 “入口”以及“……入口”一般均译作 ENTRANCE。如：“剧院入口”ENTRANCE 即可，不必译出“剧院”。“出口”以及“……出口”一般均译作 EXIT。如：“剧院出口”EXIT 即可，不必译出“剧院”。

5.2.2.3 楼层的译法。如：“1 楼 / 层”“2 楼 / 层”“3 楼 / 层”等固定缩写为 F1、F2、F3，“地下 1 层”“地下 2 层”“地下 3 层”固定缩写为 B1、B2、B3。

5.2.2.4 电梯译作 Elevator，扶梯译作 Escalator，步行楼梯译作 Stairs，电动步道译作 Moving Walkway。

5.2.2.5 前台、服务台、接待处一般译作 Reception；问询处、咨询台译作 Information。

5.2.2.6 厕所、洗手间、卫生间、盥洗室译作 Toilet 或 Restroom；涉及性别时，男厕译作 Men 或 Gents，女厕译作 Women 或 Ladies。

5.2.2.7 无障碍设施的译法，如："无障碍停车位" Accessible Parking，"无障碍电梯" Accessible Elevator。

5.2.2.8 安全保障设备应简明地译出其使用方法，如："求助按钮" Press for Help。

5.2.2.9 标有阿拉伯数字的功能设施，采用"设施名 + 阿拉伯数字"的译写方法，如："1 号门" Gate 1。

5.2.2.10 设施名称在英文中已习惯使用其缩写形式的，应采用相应的英文缩写，如："自动取款机" ATM。

5.2.3 警示及提示信息

5.2.3.1 一般性警示事项及提示信息宜用祈使句或短语表示。一般性警示事项译作 Mind... 或 Watch... 或 Beware of...，如："当心碰头" Mind Your Head，"注意脚下""当心踏空""当心台阶" Watch Your Step。

5.2.3.2 需要突出警示的警告事项使用 CAUTION 翻译，如："小心烫伤"（指开水）CAUTION // Hot Water（"//"表示应当换行，下同）。需要引起高度注意的警告事项使用 WARNING 或 DANGER 翻译，如："当心触电" DANGER // High Voltage。

5.2.4 限令禁止提示

5.2.4.1 劝阻性提示译作 Please Do Not ... 或 Thank You for Not *v*-ing，如："请勿打扰" Please Do Not Disturb。

5.2.4.2 禁止性提示译作 Do Not ... 或 No *v*-ing 或 ... Not Allowed。如："禁止吸烟" No Smoking。

5.2.4.3 需要严令禁止的提示可译作 ... Forbidden

或 ... Prohibited，如："严禁燃放烟花爆竹" Fireworks Prohibited。

5.2.5 指示指令信息

5.2.5.1 一般使用短语或祈使句翻译，如："随手关门" Close Door Behind You。

5.2.5.2 非强制性指示提醒事项，为使语气委婉，可使用 Please 引导。如："请节约用水" Please Save Water。

5.2.5.3 直接关系生命财产安全、需要强令执行的事项可以使用 Must 或 Required，如："必须戴安全帽" Head Protection Must Be Worn。

5.3 词语选用和拼写方法

5.3.1 同一事物或概念，英语国家用不同词语表达的，选择国际上更为通用的英文词语。

5.3.2 同一词语，在英语国家有不同拼写方法的，选择国际上更为通用的拼写方法。

5.3.3 同一场所中的词语选用和拼写方法应保持一致。

6. 语法格式

6.1 译文应正确使用人称、时态、单复数。

6.2 采用缩写形式应符合国际惯例。来自外来概念的中文缩略语，应使用外来概念原词的英文缩写。如："世卫组织" 应使用 WHO。

6.3 使用序数词的，可缩写为 1st、2nd 或 1st、2nd 等。

7. 书写要求

7.1 大小写

7.1.1 短语、短句字母可全部大写或者所有单词的首字母大写，如：“禁止吸烟”NO SMOKING，“禁止电动车进入电梯”No Electric Bikes Allowed。

7.1.2 短语、短句字母中4个以下字母组成的虚词全部小写。如：“出门按钮”Press to Exit。

7.1.3 长句中第一个单词、所有实义词、4个及以上字母组成的虚词、换行以后的行首词的首字母大写，如：“请随手关灯”Turn off Lights Before You Leave。如果句子或短语超过10个单词时，则按一般行文方法，句首词和专有名词的首字母大写，其余小写，但长句句尾应加上句号，如：“高血压、心脏病患者以及晕车、晕船、酗酒请勿乘坐”Visitors with hypertension, heart condition, motion sickness or excessive drinking are advised not to ride.。

7.2 标点符号

7.2.1 公示语一般不使用标点符号。但长句结尾处可用句号，分句或平行短语之间应使用逗号，如：“警示：禁止携带通信、录音、摄像设备进入会见室”WARNING: No communication, audio or video recording devices are allowed in the conference room.。

7.2.2 需要加以警示、强调时可使用感叹号。

7.3 字体

应使用相当于汉字黑体的没有衬线的等线字体，如Arial字体。

7.4 空格

7.4.1 单词内部的字母之间不空格。单词与单词之间空一格。

7.4.2 逗号、句号、感叹号、分号后空一格。双引号前后须空一格。

7.4.3 撇号（'）出现在一个单词中间时前后均不空格，如："男更衣室"Men's Locker Room。出现在词末时，后空一格，如："人才公寓"Specialists' Apartment。

7.4.4 连字符（-）前后不空格。

7.5 换行

7.5.1 一般不换行。但由警示语和警示内容两部分组成的语句，警示语和警示内容应当分行书写。

7.5.2 需要换行的，断行时应保持单词以及意义单位的完整。如："遇有火灾请勿使用电梯"Do Not Use Elevator in Case of Fire，应在 Do Not Use Elevator 和 in Case of Fire 两个意义单位之间断行（换行后 in 首字母应大写作 In）。

7.5.3 需要换行的长句排版时不得使用两端对齐。

通则英文译法示例

注：1. 以下词条在各自二级目录下按照汉语拼音字母的顺序排列（若词条以阿拉伯数字或英文字母开头，则置于表首。数字先排，从小到大；字母后排，按照字母表顺序）。

2. “〔 〕”中的内容是对英文译法的解释说明。“( )”及其所包含的内容如果是词条的组成部分应保留，如果是词条的缩写、简称或其它同义词语则可根据实际情况选择使用。

3. “/”表示“和”或者“或”，如果是词条的组成部分应保留，如果表示选择关系则根据情况选择使用。“//”表示换行。

1. 设施及服务信息

序号	中文	英文
1	1 楼 / 层、2 楼 / 层、3 楼 / 层	F1、F2、F3
2	爱心专座	Courtesy Seat
3	安全检查；安全检查通道；请接受安全检查	Security Check
4	安全须知	Safety Instructions
5	办公区	Office Area
6	保安室；门卫室；值班岗亭	Security
7	保洁室；清洁间	Cleaning Room

续表

序号	中文	英文
8	便后请冲洗	Flush After Use
9	玻璃门	Glass Door
10	布草间	Linen Room
11	布告栏；公告栏	Bulletin Board
12	步行梯；楼梯	Stairs
13	餐具	Tableware
14	餐具回收处	Leave Used Dishes Here
15	餐厅	Restaurant 或 Dining Hall
16	餐饮区	Dining Area
17	厕所；卫生间；公共厕所；洗手间；盥洗室	Toilet 或 Restroom 或 Washroom
18	茶水间	Boiled Water Room〔Room 可省略〕
19	茶歇室	Break Room
20	常设展厅	Permanent Exhibition Hall
21	车牌自动识别	License Reader
22	车位已满	Occupied
23	充电车位	EV Charger

续表

序号	中文	英文
24	出口	Exit
25	出口（表示方向）	Way Out
26	出门按钮	Press to Exit
27	厨余垃圾	Kitchen Waste
28	存包处	Lockers
29	单价	Unit Price
30	当日有效	Valid Only on Day of Issue
31	等候区	Waiting Area
32	地下 1 层、2 层、3 层	B1、B2、B3
33	地下停车场	Underground Parking
34	第三卫生间	Family Toilet
35	电动步道	Moving Walkway
36	电梯；直梯	Elevator
37	电子检票口	E-Ticket Check
38	东出口	East Exit
39	东入口	East Entrance

续表

序号	中文	英文
40	多功能室；多功能厅	Multi-Function Room 或 Multi-Function Hall
41	二十四小时营业	24-Hour Service
42	二维码	QR Code
43	访客入口	Visitor Entrance
44	非出口	No Exit
45	非水冲座便器（无需冲水）	No-Flush Toilet
46	废物箱；垃圾箱	Rubbish Bin〔Bin 可省略〕
47	扶梯；自动扶梯	Escalator
48	服务大厅	Service Hall
49	服务区	Service Area
50	复印室	Copy Room
51	工作场所营业时间	Business Hours 或 Opening Hours〔商店〕
52	工作时间	Office Hours
53	公筷	Serving Chopsticks
54	公勺	Serving Spoon
55	购票须知	Ticketing Information

续表

序号	中文	英文
56	顾客服务中心；客服中心	Customer Service Center
57	贵宾休息室	VIP Lounge
58	换票处	Ticket Change
59	会议室	Meeting Room
60	会议中心	Conference Center
61	火警电话 119	Fire Call: 119
62	货梯	Freight Elevator
63	急救中心；急救站	Emergency
64	计时停车	Metered Parking
65	价目表	Price List
66	监督投诉	Complaints
67	检票口	Ticket Check
68	节假日不办理（不营业）	Closed on Weekends and Public Holidays
69	节假日照常营业	Business as Usual on Holidays
70	紧急救护电话 120	Ambulance: 120
71	紧急求助电话 110	Emergency: 110

续表

序号	中文	英文
72	禁烟区；无烟区	Non-Smoking Area
73	可回收物（垃圾箱）	Recyclables
74	快餐厅	Snack Bar
75	快递	Express Delivery
76	快递员	Express Deliverer
77	快递中转站	Express Delivery Transfer Station
78	垃圾房	Garbage Room
79	拉	Pull
80	礼品店	Gift Store 或 Gift Shop
81	礼堂	Auditorium
82	临时停车场	Temporary Parking
83	临时展厅	Temporary Exhibition Hall
84	楼层示意图	Floor Layout
85	绿色通道	Green Channel
86	媒体中心	Media Center
87	免费存包处	Free Lockers

续表

序号	中文	英文
88	免费停车场	Free Parking
89	面部识别	Facial Recognition
90	母婴室	Baby Care Room
91	男厕所	Men 或 Gents
92	女厕所	Women 或 Ladies
93	男更衣室	Men's Locker Room
94	女更衣室	Women's Locker Room
95	内部停车场	Private Parking〔私人用〕或 Staff Parking〔员工用〕
96	派出所	Police Station
97	票务服务（售、退、补票等综合服务）	Ticket Services
98	凭票入场	Admission by Ticket Only
99	其他垃圾；不可回收物（垃圾箱）	Non-Recyclables
100	棋牌室	Chess and Cards Room〔Room 可省略〕
101	签到处	Sign-in 或 Reception
102	前台；服务台；接待处	Reception
103	清洁中	Cleaning in Progress

续表

序号	中文	英文
104	请稍候	Back Soon
105	请勿打扰	Please Do Not Disturb
106	取件处	Package Pickup
107	全日（昼夜）停车场	24-Hour Parking
108	人才公寓	Specialists' Apartment
109	人防工程出入口	Entrance and Exit of Civil Air Defense Shelter
110	入口	Entrance
111	入口（表示方向）	Way In
112	扫一扫	QR Code Scanning
113	商务中心	Business Center
114	设备维修，暂停使用	Under Repair. Temporarily out of Service
115	伸手出水	Auto Tap
116	施工期间，恕不开放	Construction in Progress // Temporarily Closed
117	试衣间	Fitting Room
118	收费标准	Rates
119	收费停车场	Pay Parking

续表

序号	中文	英文
120	收银台；收款台；缴费处	Cashier
121	手机支付服务	Mobile Phone Payment
122	售卖亭	Sales Booth
123	售票口；售票处；票务处	Ticket Office 或 Tickets
124	售罄；售完	Sold Out
125	数字安保中心	Digital Security Center
126	堂食	Dine-in
127	条形码	Barcode
128	停车场	Parking
129	停车场入口	Parking Entrance
130	停车库；停车楼	Parking Garage
131	停车时限：15 分钟	15 Minutes Parking
132	停车收费标准	Parking Rates
133	停车位；车位	Parking Space
134	投诉电话	Complaints Hotline
135	投诉邮箱	Complaints E-mail

续表

序号	中文	英文
136	推	Push
137	退票处	Refund
138	外币兑换	Currency Exchange 或 Foreign Exchange
139	外带	Take-Out
140	外卖	Food Delivery
141	卫生间请前行	Toilet Ahead
142	问讯处；咨询台	Information
143	无购物通道	No-Purchase Exit
144	无人；未使用	Vacant
145	无障碍电梯	Accessible Elevator
146	无障碍坡道	Wheelchair Accessible Ramp〔Ramp 可以省略〕
147	无障碍设施 / 残障人专用设施	Wheelchair Accessible
148	无障碍停车位	Accessible Parking
149	无障碍卫生间	Accessible Toilet
150	西餐厅	Western Restaurant
151	吸烟室	Smoking Room

续表

序号	中文	英文
152	新闻中心	Press Center
153	休息室	Lounge
154	旋转门	Revolving Door
155	样品室	Sample Room
156	医疗急救箱	First Aid Kit
157	意见箱	Suggestions & Complaints
158	应急避难场所	Emergency Shelter
159	优惠价格；特价	Discount Price
160	优惠票政策须知	Notice of Discount Tickets
161	有人；使用中	Occupied
162	预订票取票处	Ticket Claim
163	员工更衣室	Staff Locker Room
164	员工通道	Staff Only
165	阅览室；阅读区	Reading Room 或 Reading Area
166	展厅	Exhibition Hall
167	正常开放	Open

续表

序号	中文	英文
168	证件检查	ID Check
169	值班室	Duty Room
170	中餐厅	Chinese Restaurant
171	注册中心	Registration Center
172	专用车位	Reserved Parking
173	自动冲洗	Automatic Flush
174	自动充值机	Top-up Machine
175	自动检票机	Self-Service Check-in
176	自动门	Automatic Door
177	自动取款机	ATM
178	自动售货机	Vending Machine
179	自行车停放处；自行车存放处	Bicycle Parking
180	自助查询	Self-Service Information
181	自助打印	Self-Service Printing
182	自助寄存柜	Self-Service Lockers
183	自助售票区	Self-Service Ticketing

续表

序号	中文	英文
184	总价	Total Price

2. 通用警示警告信息

序号	中文	英文
1	保持安静	Please Keep Quiet
2	此区域禁止使用通信工具	No Communication Devices Allowed in This Area
3	当心触电	DANGER // High Voltage
4	当心滑坡	CAUTION // Landslide
5	当心剧毒	DANGER // Toxic Hazard
6	当心落物	Beware of Falling Objects
7	当心碰撞；谨防碰撞	Beware of Collisions
8	当心台阶；当心踏空；注意脚下	Watch Your Step
9	当心坠落	CAUTION // Do Not Go Near the Edge
10	放射物品	Radioactive Materials
11	非请勿入；员工专用；闲人免进；顾客止步	Staff Only

续表

序号	中文	英文
12	高空作业进行中，请从 2 号门进出	Overhead Work in Progress, Please Use Gate 2
13	高空作业请勿靠近	Overhead Work // Stay Away
14	高血压、心脏病患者以及晕车、晕船、酗酒请勿乘坐。	Visitors with hypertension, heart condition, motion sickness or excessive drinking are advised not to ride.
15	禁带危险品	Dangerous Articles Prohibited
16	禁用手机	No Mobile Phones
17	禁运大件物品	Do Not Carry Bulky Items
18	禁止扒门	Do Not Force Doors Open
19	禁止蹦跳	No Jumping
20	禁止泊车；禁止停车	No Parking
21	禁止超载	Do Not Exceed Weight Limit
22	禁止宠物入内	No Pets Allowed
23	禁止触摸	No Touching
24	禁止踹门	Do Not Kick Doors
25	禁止电动车进入电梯	No Electric Bikes Allowed
26	禁止毒品	Drugs Prohibited

续表

序号	中文	英文
27	禁止非机动车通行	Motor Vehicles Only
28	禁止黄、赌、毒	Pornography, Gambling and Drugs Prohibited
29	禁止将身体探出扶手外	Do Not Lean Over Handrail
30	禁止开窗	Keep Windows Closed
31	禁止跨越	No Crossing
32	禁止录像	No Video Recording
33	禁止录音	No Recording
34	禁止乱刻乱画	No Graffiti
35	禁止轮滑	No Roller Skating
36	禁止鸣笛	No Honking
37	禁止拍照摄像	No Photography or Filming
38	禁止排放污水	No Waste Water Discharge
39	禁止攀爬	No Climbing
40	禁止骑坐	No Sitting
41	禁止入内	No Entry
42	禁止手推	No Pushing

续表

序号	中文	英文
43	禁止狩猎 / 景区内禁止狩猎	No Hunting
44	禁止躺卧	No Lying Down
45	禁止跳水	No Diving
46	禁止停留（只可上下旅客）	Drop-off & Pick-up Only
47	禁止投食	No Feeding
48	禁止未成年人进入	Adults Only
49	禁止无照经营	No Unlicensed Vendors
50	禁止吸烟	No Smoking
51	禁止雪道中间停留	Do Not Stop on Ski Slope
52	禁止倚靠	No Leaning
53	禁止饮酒	No Alcohol
54	禁止饮食	No Food or Drink
55	禁止游泳	No Swimming
56	禁止张贴广告	No Posters
57	警告：防火卷帘门请勿堆物或站人	WARNING: Keep Clear of Fire Shutter at All Times
58	警示：禁止携带通信、录音、摄像设备进入会见室	WARNING: No communication, audio or video recording devices are allowed in the conference room.

续表

序号	中文	英文
59	酒后不能上船	No Boarding After Drinking
60	剧毒物品，小心作业	DANGER // Highly Toxic. Handle With Care
61	客梯严禁载货	Passengers Only
62	雷雨天气请勿在树下逗留	Do Not Stay Under a Tree in Storms
63	路面结冰	Icy Road
64	配电设施：2 米范围内严禁放置易燃物品	Power Supply Facilities: Inflammables Prohibited Within 2 Meters
65	前方弯道	Bend Ahead
66	前方有事故，请减速行驶	Accident Ahead. Slow Down.
67	清洁药剂，请勿触摸	Cleaning Agent // No Touching
68	请把垃圾进行分类投放	Please Sort Your Waste
69	请不要外放声音	Please Use Earphones
70	请出示身份证件	Please Show Your ID Card
71	请勿采摘攀折	No Picking
72	请勿打闹；请勿嬉戏打闹	Do Not Disturb Other Visitors
73	请勿倒置	Keep Upright
74	请勿逗留	No Loitering

续表

序号	中文	英文
75	请勿翻越栏杆	No Climbing Over Railings
76	请勿践踏草坪	Keep off Grass
77	请勿将手臂伸出车外	Keep Arms Inside Vehicle
78	请勿乱动开关	Do Not Touch Switch
79	请勿乱扔垃圾	No Littering
80	请勿逆行	One Way Only
81	请勿疲劳驾驶	Do Not Drive When Tired
82	请勿使用客梯载货	No Loading on Passenger Elevator
83	请勿使用闪光灯	No Flash
84	请勿手扶	No Holding
85	请勿在洗手盆内倒茶渣	No Tea Leaves in Washbasin
86	如遇火警，请勿乘坐电梯	Do Not Use Elevator in Case of Fire
87	生物危险，请勿入内	Biohazard // No Entry
88	事故多发点	Accident-Prone Area
89	水深危险禁止垂钓	Deep Water // No Angling
90	图像采集区域	This Area Is Under Video Surveillance

续表

序号	中文	英文
91	外来车辆禁止入内； 社会车辆禁止入内	Authorized Vehicles Only
92	危险物品	Hazardous Materials
93	卧床请勿吸烟	Please Do Not Smoke in Bed
94	小心玻璃	CAUTION // Glass
95	小心车辆	CAUTION // Moving Vehicles
96	小心地滑 （地面建筑材质本身较光滑）	CAUTION // Slippery Surface
97	小心地滑（雨雪天气路面湿滑）	CAUTION // Slippery When Wet
98	小心落水	WARNING // Deep Water
99	小心门外行人	CAUTION // Open Slowly
100	小心碰头	Watch Your Head
101	小心烫伤（指开水）	CAUTION // Hot Water
102	小心斜坡；注意坡度	CAUTION // Ramp
103	小心障碍	Beware of Obstruction
104	严禁踩踏	No Stepping
105	严禁超速	No Speeding
106	严禁戏水	No Wading

续表

序号	中文	英文
107	严禁携带易燃、易爆、有毒物等违禁品	Flammable, Explosive, Poisonous and Other Illegal Materials Strictly Prohibited
108	严禁中途下车	No Drop-off Between Stops
109	有害气体！注意安全	CAUTION // Toxic Gases
110	注意安全，请勿靠近	CAUTION // Keep Away

3. 通用指示说明信息

序号	中文	英文
1	1 米以下儿童谢绝入内	No Admittance for Children Under 1 Meter
2	1 米以下儿童须家长陪同乘坐	Children Under 1 Meter Must Be Accompanied by an Adult
3	1.2 米以下儿童免票	Free for Children Under 1.2 Meters
4	必须戴安全帽	Head Protection Must Be Worn
5	必须戴防护眼镜	Safety Goggles Required
6	必须佩戴手套	Gloves Required
7	必须系安全带（穿戴式安全带）	Safety Belt Must Be Worn
8	参观车辆入口	Visitor Vehicle Access

续表

序号	中文	英文
9	餐具已消毒	Sterilized
10	出口请慢行	Slow Down at Exit
11	此路不通	No Through Road 或 Dead End
12	此门已经关闭请走其他通道	Please Use Another Door
13	待更换	To Be Replaced
14	待修	To Be Repaired
15	电梯运行时请站在安全线内	Please Stand Behind the Safety Line
16	电梯在本层不停	No Elevator Access on This Floor
17	儿童搭乘须有成人陪同	Children Must Be Accompanied by an Adult
18	防止长裙、鞋带等卷入	Keep Loose Clothing and Shoe String Clear of Steps and Sides
19	访客请登记	Visitor Registration
20	扶梯乘梯须知	Instructions on Escalator Use
21	贵重物品请自行妥善保管	Please Keep Your Valuables With You
22	行动不便者请走旁门	Those With Special Needs May Use the Side Door
23	节约能源随手断电	Energy Saving Reminder: Power Down When Not Using
24	紧急情况下请按此键	Press in Emergency

续表

序号	中文	英文
25	进入实验区，请穿好工作服	Lab Coats Required in This Area
26	老人、孕妇、怀抱婴儿、不便人士优先	Priority to elderly, expectant mothers, baby holders, and people with special needs.
27	绿化养护中	Green Maintenance in Progress
28	清洁中请勿入内	Cleaning in Progress // No Entry
29	请“扫一扫”上方二维码	Please Scan the QR Code
30	请爱护古迹 / 请保护古迹	Please Show Respect for Historic Sites
31	请爱护花草树木	Please Show Respect for Trees and Plants
32	请爱护环境	Please Show Respect for Our Environment
33	请爱护书籍	Please Handle Books With Care
34	请爱护文物 / 保护文物	Please Show Respect for Cultural Relics
35	请把手机调至静音	Please Mute Your Mobile Phone
36	请保管好个人物品	Please Do Not Leave Your Personal Belongings Unattended
37	请乘坐本电梯至 8 层	Elevator to 8th Floor
38	请出示读者证	Please Show Your Library Card
39	请出示证件	Please Show Your ID
40	请关闭手机	Please Switch off Your Mobile Phone

续表

序号	中文	英文
41	请及时关空调	Please Turn off Air Conditioner Before You Leave
42	请节约用水	Please Save Water
43	请节约用纸	Do Not Waste Paper
44	请保存好购物凭证	Please Keep Your Receipt
45	请穿好救生衣	Please Wear Life Jacket
46	请从 1 号门出入	Please Use Gate 1
47	请佩戴口罩	Please Keep Mask on
48	请绕行	Detour
49	请刷卡	Swipe Card Here
50	请随手关灯	Turn off Lights Before You Leave
51	请随手关门	Close Door Behind You
52	请握住扶手	Please Hold Handrail
53	请系好安全带	Fasten Seat Belt
54	请下车推行	Please Walk Your Bicycle
55	请在此等候	Please Wait Here
56	请在此开发票	Request Your Invoice Here

续表

序号	中文	英文
57	请在此排队；请排队等候	Line Up Here 或 Please Wait in Line
58	请在黄线外等候	Please Wait Behind Yellow Line
59	请在前门上车	Please Get on at Front Door
60	请在后门下车	Please Get off at Rear Door
61	请找工作人员协助	Please Ask Staff for Assistance
62	请照看好老人、儿童	Do Not Leave Elderly or Children Unaccompanied
63	请注意交通信号灯	Watch for Traffic Lights
64	请自觉维护场内卫生环境	Please Keep This Area Clean
65	请走步梯	Please Use Stairs
66	请走旋转门	Please Use Revolving Door
67	请尊重少数民族习俗	Please Show Respect for Ethnic Customs
68	请遵守场内秩序	Please Observe Rules of Etiquette
69	求助电话	Emergency Call
70	扫码取件	Scan to Access
71	扫码支付	Scan to Pay
72	上下楼梯请靠右	Keep Right

续表

序号	中文	英文
73	食品饮料	Food and Beverages
74	易碎物品请轻拿轻放	FRAGILE // Handle With Care
75	有毒垃圾回收	Toxic Waste Collection
76	有佛事活动，请绕行	Service in Progress // Please Take Another Route
77	逾期交费	Overdue Payment
78	阅后请放回原处	Please Reshelve Books Where You Found Them
79	阅览室内请保持安静	Please Keep Quiet
80	允许拍照留念	Photos Allowed
81	找零请当面点清	Please Check Your Change Before You Leave
82	中场休息	Halftime
83	注意归还日期，按时还书	Please Return Books on Time

4. 消防安全提示信息

序号	中文	英文
1	安全出口	EXIT 或 Exit

续表

序号	中文	英文
2	安全出口，严禁锁闭	Emergency Exit // Keep Unlocked
3	安全楼梯	Emergency Stairs
4	常闭式防火门，请保持关闭	Fire Door // Keep Closed
5	常开式防火门，严禁锁闭	Fire Door // Keep Unlocked
6	当心爆炸物	Explosive Materials // Handle With Care
7	当心氧化物	Oxidizing Substances // Handle With Care
8	当心易燃物	Flammable Materials // Handle With Care
9	防洪通道，请勿占用	Flood Control Channel // Keep Clear
10	防火卷帘按钮	Fire Shutter Button
11	防火卷帘门	Fire Shutters
12	防火卷帘下严禁堆放杂物	Fire Shutters // Keep Clear
13	防火门	Fire Door
14	非紧急情况勿动	Emergency Use Only
15	火警时，击碎玻璃	In case of fire, smash glass cover and press emergency button.
16	火情警报；火情警报器	Fire Alarm
17	紧急出口	Emergency Exit

续表

序号	中文	英文
18	紧急出口，保持通畅	Emergency Exit // Keep Clear
19	紧急情况下请击碎玻璃	Break Glass in Emergency
20	紧急疏散集合地	Evacuation Assembly Area
21	禁止放置易燃物	No Flammables
22	禁止明火作业	No Open Flames
23	禁止燃放烟花爆竹	No Fireworks 或 Fireworks Prohibited
24	禁止烟火	No Smoking or Open Flames
25	灭火器	Fire Extinguisher
26	您所在位置	You Are Here
27	排烟口，严禁遮挡	Smoke Vent // Keep Clear
28	手动报警按钮，火灾时请按下，非紧急情况勿动	Emergency Button // Press in Case of Fire // Emergency Use Only
29	手提式灭火器	Portable Fire Extinguisher
30	疏散路线	Evacuation Route
31	疏散引导箱	Evacuation Equipment
32	送风口，严禁遮挡	Air Vent // Keep Clear
33	逃生路线	Escape Route

续表

序号	中文	英文
34	推车式灭火器	Wheeled Fire Extinguisher
35	消防泵房，闲人免进	Fire Pumps // Staff Only
36	消防车	Fire Engine
37	消防疏散示意图	Fire Evacuation Plan
38	消防栓	Fire Hydrant
39	消防通道	Fire Lane
40	消防通道，不得占用	Fire Lane // Keep Clear
41	消防应急面罩	Fire Mask
42	消防专用开关	Fire Fighter's Switch
43	烟雾报警器	Smoke Detector
44	严禁圈占消火栓	Keep Clear of Fire Hydrant
45	应急照明灯	Emergency Light
46	注意防火	Beware of Fire Hazard
47	注意防火，请勿乱扔烟蒂	Do Not Discard Cigarette Butts on the Ground

二、道路交通

Part 2 Transportation

1. 范围

本部分规定了南京市交通服务领域英文译写的相关术语和定义、译写要求和方法等。

本部分适用于南京市道路交通信息、设施服务信息、交通运输服务信息的英文译写。

2. 规范性引用文件

应用本部分内容需参考如下文件。如文件注明日期，则仅注日期的版本适用于本文件。如文件未注日期，则其最新版本（包括所有的修改单）适用于本部分。

GB 17733 地名 标志

GB 5768.2—2009 道路交通标志和标线（第 2 部分：道路交通标志）

GB/T 10001（所有部分）标志用公共信息图形符号

GB/T 917 公路路线标识规则和国道编号

GB/T 30240.1—2013 公共服务领域英文译写规范（第 1 部分：通则）

GB/T 30240.2—2017 公共服务领域英文译写规范（第 2 部分：交通）

DB32/T 1446.2—2009 公共场所英文译写规范（第 2 部分：交通）

3. 术语和定义

下列术语和定义适用于本部分。

3.1 道路交通信息 road traffic information

设置在公路、城市道路以及虽在单位管辖范围但允许公众通行的地方，为机动车、非机动车驾驶人员以及行人提供的交通信息。

3.2 公共运输信息 public transportation information

对公众开放，提供航空、铁路、轮船、轨道、公共汽车、出租车等的客运服务信息。

4. 译写要求

4.1 交通服务领域公共场所中文标识在 GB/T 10001.1 中已经规定了相应的图形符号时，应首先按照标准的规定使用公共信息图形符号。使用国际通用标识符号或图标的，可不提供英文译写。

4.2 交通服务公共场所中文标识采用英文译写时，英文单词的大小写应符合本指南第 1 部分的规定；采用汉语拼音标注时，拼写应符合 GB/T 16159 的规定。

5. 译写方法

5.1 道路交通信息

5.1.1 地名通名

5.1.1.1 作为地名的路、街、巷等路名牌信息根据 GB 17733—2008 采用汉语拼音字母拼写形式。

5.1.1.2 在对外交流和服务场合，路、街、巷等通名可采用英文直接翻译，英文单词首字母大写，其余小写。

5.1.1.3 街

大道、大街译作 Avenue 或 Ave.，如：“玄武大道” Xuanwu Avenue。街、道译作 Street 或 St.，如：“府西街” Fuxi Street。小街、条、巷、夹道译作 Alley 或 Lane，如：“饮马巷” Yinma Alley。

5.1.1.4 路

路译作 Road 或 Rd.，如：“虎踞路” Huju Road。高速公路译作 Expressway，如：“宁杭高速” Ninghang Expressway。城市道路中的高架（快速路）译作 Elevated Expressway，如：“江北大道快速路” Jiangbeidadao Elevated Expressway。公路译作 Highway，如：“宁丹公路” Ningdan Highway。其他通名的译法如下，立体交叉口译作 Interchange，如：“新庄立交” Xinzhuang Interchange。隧道译作 Tunnel，如：“万景园隧道” Wanjingyuan Tunnel。桥译作 Bridge，如：“南京长江大桥” Nanjing Yangtze River Bridge。

5.1.1.5 地铁、公交站名中的地名通名采用汉语拼音字母拼写，与专名连写，后重复意译，如：“上海路站” SHANGHAILU Station，“笆斗山站” BADOUSHAN Station。

5.1.2 地名专名

5.1.2.1 地名专名通常采用汉语拼音标注，首字母大写。

5.1.2.2 专有名词作为路名时，采用汉语拼音，如：“鼓楼街” Gulou Street。其他场合可翻译成英文，如：“鼓楼” Drum Tower。

5.1.2.3 指示以地区名称等专名命名的街道或立交桥时，地区名用汉语拼音，街道或立交桥翻译成英文，如：“应天大街高架” Yingtiandajie Elevated Expressway，“赛虹桥立交”Saihongqiao Interchange。

5.1.2.4　地铁、公交车站名称

地铁、公交站名中的地名专名和通名全部采用大写汉语拼音，如：“金马路”JINMALU。但场馆、大学和商店等名称作为站名时可翻译成英文，如：“南大仙林校区” NJU XIANLIN CAMPUS。

5.2　公共运输信息

5.2.1　飞机场、火车站、轮船码头（港口）名称用作地名时，应符合 GB/T 30240.1—2013 中第 4.1.3 条的相关要求。对外服务中需要用英文予以解释的，飞机场译作 Airport，火车站译作 Railway Station，大型港口译作 Port，客运码头、轮渡站译作 Passenger Dock，货运码头译作 Freight Dock，装卸码头译作 Loading/Unloading Dock。

5.2.2　轨道交通和公共汽车站点名称用作地名时，应符合 GB/T 30240.1—2013 中第 4.1.3 条的相关要求。对外服务中需要用英文予以解释的，轨道交通（包括地铁和轻轨）译作 Metro，轨道交通站点译作 Station，换乘站译作 Transfer Station，公共汽车始发站和终点站译作 Terminal 或 Station，公共汽车沿途站点译作 Stop。

5.3　其他道路交通服务信息

5.3.1　道路交通指示标识应遵守相关法律法规，符合相关行业有关规定。

5.3.2　其他交通道路服务信息的英文译写应符合 GB/T 30240.1—2013 和 GB/T 30240.2—2017 的规定。采用英文直接翻译时，应符合国际通用惯例。

道路交通英文译法示例

注：1. 以下词条在各自二级目录下按照汉语拼音字母的顺序排列（若词条以阿拉伯数字或英文字母开头，则置于表首。数字先排，从小到大；字母后排，按照字母表顺序）。

2. “〔 〕”中的内容是对英文译法的解释说明。“（ ）”及其所包含的内容如果是词条的组成部分应保留，如果是词条的缩写、简称或其它同义词语则可根据实际情况选择使用。

3. “/”表示“和”或者“或”，如果是词条的组成部分应保留，如果表示选择关系则根据情况选择使用。“//”表示换行。

1. 道路交通设施信息

序号	中文	英文
1	避险车道	Truck Escape Ramp 或 Runaway Truck Ramp
2	标线	Marking
3	步行道	Walkway
4	步行街	Pedestrian Street
5	仓库	Warehouse
6	超车道	Overtaking Lane 或 Passing Lane
7	车辆上下客区	Passenger Pick-up & Drop-off Area〔Area 可省略〕

续表

序号	中文	英文
8	城市道路	Urban Road
9	出租车专用停车位	Taxi Parking Only 或 Taxis Only
10	次干路	Sub-Arterial Road
11	村庄	Village
12	大型车	Heavy Vehicles
13	大道；大街	Avenue
14	大客车停车位	Bus Parking Only 或 Buses Only
15	大客车专用出 / 入口	Bus Exit / Entrance
16	大型车道	Heavy Vehicle Lane 或 Heavy Vehicles〔用于 Lane 可省略的场合〕
17	堤坝路	Embankment Road
18	地面道路	Ground-Level Road
19	电子收费	Electronic Toll Collection 或 ETC
20	渡口	Ferry
21	非机动车	Non-Motor Vehicles
22	非机动车专用停车位	Non-Motor Vehicle Parking Only 或 Non-Motor Vehicles Only
23	分拨中心	Allocation Center

续表

序号	中文	英文
24	服务区	Service Area
25	辅路	Side Road
26	干线公路	Trunk Highway
27	高架道路	Elevated Road 或 Elevated Highway
28	高架桥	Overpass〔指城市中的高架桥〕或 Viaduct〔指横跨河流或山谷的高架桥〕
29	高速公路	Expressway
30	公共停车场	Public Parking
31	公路	Highway
32	国道	National Highway 或 National Road
33	货车	Trucks
34	拖拉机	Tractors
35	货运枢纽	Cargo Terminal
36	机动车	Motor Vehicles
37	集装箱堆场	Container Yard
38	集装箱中转站	Container Transfer Station
39	计时停车	Hourly Parking 或 Metered Parking

续表

序号	中文	英文
40	加气站	Natural Gas Station
41	加油站	Petrol Station
42	减速带；减速路面；减速丘	Speed Bumps 或 Speed Humps
43	交叉路口	Crossroads 或 Intersection
44	交通监控设备	Traffic Surveillance
45	交通信号灯	Traffic Lights
46	街；道	Street
47	紧急停车带	Emergency Stop Area
48	卡车停靠点	Truck Parking Only 或 Trucks Only
49	跨线桥	Overpass
50	立交桥（车行）	Highway Interchange
51	临时停车位	Temporary Parking
52	路	Road
53	路侧划线停车位	Roadside Parking
54	免费停车场	Free Parking
55	内部停车场	Private Parking〔私人用〕或 Staff Parking〔员工用〕

续表

序号	中文	英文
56	爬坡车道	Climbing Lane
57	配货区	Distribution Area
58	配送中心	Distribution Center
59	桥梁	Bridge
60	全日停车场（昼夜服务）	24-Hour Parking
61	让车道；错车道	Passing Bay
62	绕城公路；环路	Beltway 或 Ring Road
63	人行道	Sidewalk 或 Pedestrians
64	人行横道	Pedestrian Crossing
65	人行天桥	Footbridge
66	社会车辆出 / 入口	Private Vehicle Entrance / Exit
67	省道	Provincial Highway 或 Provincial Road
68	收费公路	Tollway 或 Toll Road
69	收费停车场	Pay Parking
70	收费站	Toll Station 或 Toll Gate
71	隧道	Tunnel

续表

序号	中文	英文
72	铁路道口	Railway Crossing
73	网约车上车点	Online Car Hailing Pick-up Area
74	物流园区	Logistics Park
75	物流中心	Logistics Center
76	县道	County Highway 或 County Road
77	巷；条；小街；夹道	Alley
78	小型车	Light Vehicles
79	小型车道	Light Vehicle Lane
80	小型车停车场	Car Parking
81	小型车专用出 / 入口	Light Vehicle Exit / Entrance
82	校车停靠站点	School Bus Stop
83	休息区	Rest Area
84	应急避难设施（或场所）	Emergency Shelter
85	应急车道	Emergency Lane
86	支路	Access Road
87	主干路	Arterial Road

续表

序号	中文	英文
88	专属停车位	Reserved Parking
89	综合货运站	Comprehensive Cargo Services

2. 交通运输服务信息

（1）航空客运

序号	中文	英文
1	2 号登机口	Gate 2
2	办理国际登机手续	International Check-in
3	办理国内登机手续	Domestic Check-in
4	出发大厅	Departures Hall
5	出发航班信息	Departures Information〔Information 可省略〕
6	到达大厅	Arrivals Hall
7	到达航班信息	Arrivals Information〔Information 可省略〕
8	到达时间	Arrival Time
9	登机	Boarding

续表

序号	中文	英文
10	登机口	Gate
11	登机桥	Boarding Bridge
12	登机信息	Boarding Information
13	第 2 航站楼	Terminal 2
14	电子机票	Electronic Tickets 或 E-Tickets
15	公务舱；商务舱	Business Class
16	公务舱候机室	Business Class Lounge〔Lounge 可省略〕
17	柜台关闭	Counter Closed
18	贵宾通道	VIP Passage〔Passage 可省略〕
19	国际、港澳台航班	International and Hong Kong / Macao / Taiwan Flights
20	国际航班通道	International Flight Passage 或 International Flights〔用于 Passage 可省略的场合〕
21	国际机场	International Airport
22	国际转机	International Transfer
23	国内航班通道	Domestic Flight Passage 或 Domestic Flights〔用于 Passage 可省略的场合〕
24	国内转机	Domestic Transfer
25	过站旅客；过境旅客	Transit Passengers

续表

序号	中文	英文
26	航班号	Flight No.
27	航班信息	Flight Information
28	航空货运	Air Freight
29	航站楼	Terminal
30	航站楼出发层平面图	Departure Level Map
31	航站楼到达层平面图	Arrival Level Map
32	候机区域	Waiting Area
33	换乘、中转	Transfer
34	机舱服务员专用通道	Crew Passage 或 Crew Only〔用于 Passage 可省略的场合〕
35	机场	Airport
36	机场巴士	Airport Bus 或 Shuttle Bus
37	机场高速	Airport Expressway
38	经济舱	Economy Class
39	经停	Transit
40	经停航班	Stopover Flight
41	救生衣	Life Vest 或 Life Jacket

续表

序号	中文	英文
42	民航售票	Airline Tickets 或 Ticketing
43	起飞前 40 分钟停止办理乘机手续	Check-in Closes 40 Minutes Before Departure
44	起飞时间	Departure Time
45	请出示登机牌和身份证件	Please Show Your Boarding Pass and ID
46	请留意您乘坐航班的登机时间，以免误机	Please Pay Attention to Your Boarding Time
47	停机坪摆渡车	Airside Transfer Bus 或 Apron Bus
48	停止办票	Check-in Closed
49	停止登机	Boarding Closed
50	头等舱	First Class
51	头等舱 / 商务舱服务	First / Business Class Services
52	头等舱候机室	First Class Lounge〔Lounge 可省略〕
53	氧气罩	Oxygen Mask
54	应急门	Escape Door 或 Emergency Door
55	优先登机	Priority Boarding
56	直达航班	Direct Flight
57	值机柜台；办票柜台；办理乘机手续柜台	Check-in Counter〔Counter 可省略〕

续表

序号	中文	英文
58	值机区域；办理登机区	Check-in Area〔Area 可省略〕
59	中转联程	Connecting Flights
60	转机；换乘	Transfer 或 Flight Connections
61	转机旅客	Transfer Passengers
62	自动步行道	Automatic Walkway 或 Moving Walkway
63	自助值机；乘机手续自助办理机	Self Check-in

（2）铁路客运

序号	中文	英文
1	餐车	Dining Car
2	城际列车	Inter-City Railway
3	乘务员室	Crew Office 或 Crew Only
4	乘务员席位	Crew Seat 或 Crew Only〔用于 Seat 可省略的场合〕
5	单程	One-Way
6	到达出口	Arrivals 或 Arrival Exit
7	动车组列车；动车	Electric Multiple Units (EMU) Train

续表

序号	中文	英文
8	二等座	Second Class
9	复兴号	Fuxing Bullet Train
10	高速铁路；高铁	High-Speed Railway
11	和谐号	Hexie Bullet Train
12	候补	Waitlist
13	候车楼；候车厅	Passenger Terminal 或 Waiting Hall
14	火车售票	Railway Tickets 或 Train Tickets
15	火车站	Railway Station
16	货运列车	Freight Train
17	货运站	Freight Station
18	紧急制动	Emergency Braking
19	客运站	Passenger Station
20	快速列车	Fast Train
21	临时旅客列车	Extra Passenger Train
22	旅游列车	Tourist Train
23	普客列车	Regular Passenger Train

续表

序号	中文	英文
24	普快列车	Fast Passenger Train
25	普通席	Economy Class
26	软卧车厢	Soft Sleeper 或 Soft Berth
27	软座车厢	Soft Seat
28	商务座	Business Class
29	商务座候车室	Business Class Waiting Lounge
30	特快列车	Express Train
31	铁路货运	Rail Freight
32	往返	Round-Trip
33	一等座	First Class
34	硬卧车厢	Hard Sleeper 或 Hard Berth
35	硬座车厢	Hard Seat
36	邮政车	Mail Car
37	预售 15 日内全国各线车票	15-Day Advance Booking for All Destinations
38	直达特快列车	Non-Stop Express Train
39	智能动车组	Intelligent Electric Multiple Units (EMU)

续表

序号	中文	英文
40	中转换乘	Transfer

（3）轮船客运

序号	中文	英文
1	渡船	Ferry Boat
2	港口	Port
3	观光船码头	Sightseeing Cruise Dock
4	候船室	Waiting Room
5	货运码头	Freight Dock
6	客运码头	Passenger Dock
7	轮船售票	Boat Tickets
8	码头	Dock
9	装卸码头	Loading/Unloading Dock

（4）轨道交通客运

序号	中文	英文
1	地铁	Metro
2	地铁 2 号线	Metro Line 2
3	地铁车站	Metro Station 或 Station
4	地铁换乘查询	Metro Transfer Information
5	地铁换乘站	Transfer Station
6	地铁智能导向综合信息系统	Metro Service Information Query System
7	地铁终点站	Terminus 或 Terminal
8	换乘 4 号线	Transfer to Line 4
9	轻轨	Light Rail
10	请在安全线内候车，车门未完全打开或关闭，不得触摸车门。	Please stand behind the safety line. Do not touch the door before it is fully opened or closed.

（5）公共汽车客运

序号	中文	英文
1	班车乘车地点	Shuttle Bus Pick-up Point 或 Commuter Bus Pick-up Point
2	班车服务	Shuttle Bus Services 或 Commuter Bus Services

续表

序号	中文	英文
3	长途汽车	Coach
4	长途汽车站	Coach Station 或 Coach Terminal
5	公共汽车	Bus
6	公共汽车路线图	Bus Route
7	公交换乘	Bus Transfer
8	公交换乘信息	Bus Transfer Information
9	公交枢纽站	Public Transport Hub
10	公交信息	Public Transport Information
11	公交站点	Bus Stop
12	公交中心站	Central Bus Station
13	紧急手柄（指拉手）	Emergency Handle
14	请等车停稳后再下	Please do not get off until the vehicle comes to a complete stop.
15	有轨电车	Tramcar
16	直达车	Non-Stop Bus〔公共汽车〕或 Non-Stop Coach〔长途汽车〕

（6）出租车客运

序号	中文	英文
1	出租车	Taxi
2	出租车待客区	Taxi Stand 或 Taxi
3	出租车发票	Taxi Receipt
4	出租车起步价	Base Fare
5	出租车调度站	Taxi Dispatching Station
6	出租车投诉电话	Taxi Service Complaints Hotline
7	出租车预约电话	Taxi Booking
8	共享单车	Shared Bike
9	共享单车调度站	Shared Bike Dispatching Station
10	共享单车站点	Bike-Sharing Station
11	共享单车租金	Bike-Sharing Rental Fee
12	上客点	Passenger Pick-up
13	网约车	Online Car Hailing

（7）通用类

序号	中文	英文
1	IC 卡查询业务	IC Card Inquiry Service
2	安全检查	Security Check
3	办理临时身份证明	Temporary-ID Service
4	北 1 出口	North Exit 1
5	边防检查	Immigration Inspection
6	边检民警为您服务	Immigration Officers at Your Service
7	边检咨询	Immigration Information
8	超大行李	Oversized Baggage
9	超规行李登记	Oversized / Overweight Baggage Check-in
10	超重行李	Overweight Baggage
11	车票	Ticket
12	乘客服务中心	Passenger Service Center
13	乘客专用	For Passengers Only
14	出境登记卡	Departure Card
15	出站检查；出站验票	Exit Ticket Check

续表

序号	中文	英文
16	大件行李	Large Baggage
17	第 1 通道	Passage 1
18	动植物检疫	Animal and Plant Quarantine
19	儿童票适用身高：____ 米—____ 米	Height Limits for Children's Tickets: ____ m - ____ m
20	方向引导	Direction Guide
21	公共交通卡充值	Top-up // Public Transportation Card Only
22	购票须知	Ticketing Information
23	红色通道（有申报物品）	Red Channel // Goods to Declare
24	会合大厅	Waiting Lounge 或 Waiting Hall
25	货物查询	Freight Inquiry
26	货物检查	Freight Check
27	货物交运	Freight Check-in
28	货物提取	Freight Collection
29	货物托运	Freight Consignment
30	稽查管理	Inspection Management
31	急救站；医疗急救室	First Aid Station〔Station 可省略〕

续表

序号	中文	英文
32	检票通道	Ticket Check Passage
33	交通卡余额	Card Balance
34	交通卡原额	Previous Card Balance
35	交通枢纽周边示意图	Surrounding Area Map
36	交通信息查询机	Inquiry Machine
37	今日运营已结束	Closed
38	进站检票；检票口	Ticket Check
39	禁止携带托运放射性及磁性物品	Radioactive and Magnetic Materials Prohibited 或 No Radioactive or Magnetic Materials
40	禁止携带托运易燃及易爆物品	Flammable and Explosive Materials Prohibited 或 No Flammables or Explosives
41	禁止携带武器及仿真武器	Weapons and Simulated Weapons Prohibited 或 No Weapons or Simulated Weapons 或 No Weapons or Imitation Weapons
42	禁止倚靠车门	Do Not Lean on
43	口岸限定区域	Restricted Area
44	列车门蜂鸣声响，请勿上下列车。	Do not get on or off the train when the door-bell buzzes.
45	列车门关闭，请立刻退到安全线以内。	Stay Behind the Yellow Line When the Door Is Closing.
46	旅客出口	Passenger Exit

续表

序号	中文	英文
47	旅客等候区	Passenger Waiting Area
48	旅客通道，请勿滞留	Please Keep Passage Clear 或 Busy Passage // Keep Clear
49	绿色通道（无申报物品）	Green Channel // Nothing to Declare
50	门灯闪烁时禁止上下车。	Do not get on or off the train when the door-light is flashing.
51	免费行李重量	Baggage Allowance
52	末班车	Last Train〔火车〕或 Last Bus〔公共汽车〕
53	母婴休息室	Baby-Care Lounge
54	南 1 出口	South Exit 1
55	逆时针方向扳动手柄 90 度	Turn the Handle 90 Degrees Counterclockwise
56	票价	Fares
57	票务服务	Ticket Services 或 Ticketing
58	凭证通行	Permit Required
59	前方到站；下一站	Next Station〔轨道交通站点〕或 Next Stop〔公交车站点〕
60	切勿倒置（指货物、行李的摆放）	Keep Upright
61	切勿挤压（指货物、行李的摆放）	Fragile
62	请到售票处处理	Please Go to the Ticket Office for Help

续表

序号	中文	英文
63	请您别遗忘放在手推车上的物品	Please Do Not Leave Behind Any Belonging on Cart
64	请您向下按手柄，松开刹车后推行	Press Down Handle to Move the Cart
65	请您由此进入依次候检	Please Line Up Here
66	请维护好车厢的清洁卫生	Thank You for Helping Us Keep This Bus Clean〔公共汽车〕或 Thank You for Helping Us Keep This Car Clean〔火车〕
67	请勿将行李手推车推入自动扶梯	No Baggage Cart Allowed on Escalator
68	请勿将头手伸出窗外	Keep Head and Hands Inside
69	请勿开窗	Please Do Not Open Window
70	请勿向窗外扔东西	Do Not Throw Anything Out of Window
71	请勿阻止车门关闭	Keep Clear of Closing Doors
72	请选择要查询的线路	Please Select Line
73	请在黄线外等候	Please Wait Behind the Yellow Line
74	请自觉遵守乘车秩序	Please Observe Passenger Rules
75	入境登记卡	Arrival Cards
76	设施服务时间	Service Hours
77	始发站	Departure Station

续表

序号	中文	英文
78	手提行李规格	Size and Weight Limits for Carry-on Baggage
79	首 / 末班车发班时间	Time for First / Last Train of This Line
80	首班车	First Train〔火车〕或 First Bus〔公共汽车〕
81	售票口；售票处；票务处	Ticket Office 或 Tickets
82	售全线票；通售所有站点车票	Tickets for All Stations
83	枢纽站	Junction Station
84	送客止步	Passengers Only
85	团队集合点	Group Gathering Point
86	团队通道	Groups Passage〔Passage 可省略〕
87	外国人通道	Non-Chinese Nationals Passage〔Passage 可省略〕
88	外交礼遇通道	Diplomatic Personnel Passage〔Passage 可省略〕
89	往返票	Round-Trip Ticket
90	为了您和他人的乘车安全，请不要携带易燃、易爆、易碎和笨重物品乘车。	For your safety and the safety of others, please do not carry on board any flammable, explosive, fragile or heavy articles.
91	勿放潮湿处（指货物、行李的摆放）	Store in Dry Place
92	下车请勿忘物品	Please Do Not Leave Behind Your Belongings

续表

序号	中文	英文
93	先下后上	Yield to Alighting Passengers
94	限紧急时使用	For Emergency Use Only
95	小心脚下间隙落差；注意站台缝隙	Mind the Gap
96	小心碰撞	Beware of Collision
97	信用卡支付	We Accept Credit Cards
98	休息处	Rest Area 或 Lounge
99	休息大厅；等候大厅	Waiting Hall
100	行李安检	Baggage Security Check
101	行李安检通道	Baggage Check
102	行李查询	Baggage Inquiry
103	行李寄存	Baggage Deposit
104	行李寄存须知	Notice of Baggage Deposit
105	行李提取	Baggage Claim
106	行李托运	Baggage Check-in
107	行李专用，请勿载人（行李手推车用）	For Baggage Only // No Riding
108	严禁携带危险品	Dangerous Articles Prohibited

续表

序号	中文	英文
109	液态物品	Liquids
110	暂停售票	Temporarily Closed
111	站台；月台	Platform
112	证照检查	ID Check
113	执勤岗	Duty Post
114	中国公民通道（含香港、澳门及台湾居民）	Chinese Nationals (Including Residents of Hong Kong, Macao and Taiwan)
115	终点站	Destination 或 Terminus
116	驻站民警室	Police Office〔Office 可省略〕
117	自动寄包柜	Self-Service Locker
118	自动检票	Automatic Check-in

3. 交通警示指示说明信息

序号	中文	英文
1	保持车距	Keep Distance 或 Keep Safe Distance
2	避让行人	Yield to Pedestrians

续表

序号	中文	英文
3	超限检测站	Weigh Station
4	车道封闭	Lane Closed
5	车距确认	Check Your Distance
6	车辆绕行	Detour
7	除公共汽车外（其他车辆不得进入或停靠）	Buses Only
8	此路不通	No Through Road 或 Dead End
9	道路封闭	Road Closed
10	道路交通信息	Traffic Information
11	掉头车道	U-Turn Lane〔Lane 可省略〕
12	掉头和左转合用车道	Left or U-Turn Lane〔Lane 可省略〕
13	东、南、西、北	E, S, W, N
14	东南、东北、西南、西北	SE, NE, SW, NW
15	陡坡	Steep Descent Ahead
16	反向弯路	Reverse Curve
17	非机动车车道	Non-Motor Vehicle Lane〔Lane 可省略〕
18	服务区预告	Service Area Ahead

续表

序号	中文	英文
19	公共汽车优先	Bus Priority
20	公交路线专用车道	Bus Lane 或 Buses Only〔用于 Lane 可省略的场合〕
21	行人、自行车横过马路请使用天桥	Pedestrians and Cyclists May Cross by Footbridge
22	行人绕行	Pedestrians Detour
23	环岛行驶	Roundabout
24	会车让行	Give Way to Oncoming Vehicles
25	会车先行	Priority Over Oncoming Vehicles
26	机动车车道	Motor Vehicle Lane〔Lane 可省略〕
27	急弯路	Sharp Bend 或 Sharp Curve
28	计重收费	Toll-by-Weight
29	减速让行	YIELD
30	解除禁止超车	END // No-Overtaking 或 End of No-Overtaking Zone
31	解除限制速度：____ 千米 / 小时	End // ____ km/h Speed Limit
32	紧急电话	Emergency Call
33	谨防追尾	Beware of Rear End Collision
34	禁止超车	No Overtaking

续表

序号	中文	英文
35	禁止超高	Do Not Exceed Height Limit
36	禁止超速	No Speeding 或 Do Not Exceed Speed Limit
37	禁止超载	Do Not Overload 或 Do Not Exceed Weight Limit
38	禁止大型客车驶入	No Large Buses
39	禁止小型客车驶入	No Minibuses
40	禁止掉头	No U-Turn
41	禁止非机动车驶入	Motor Vehicles Only 或 No Entry for Non-Motor Vehicles
42	禁止机动车驶入	No Motor Vehicles
43	禁止酒后驾车	Do Not Drink and Drive 或 Driving After Drinking Is Prohibited by Law
44	禁止鸣笛	No Honking 或 No Horns
45	禁止疲劳驾驶	Do Not Drive When Tired
46	禁止停车	No Stopping 或 No Stopping at Any Time
47	禁止通道两侧停车	No Parking on Either Side
48	禁止通行	Do Not Enter 或 No Entry
49	禁止外来车辆驶入	Staff Vehicles Only
50	禁止向右转弯	No Right Turn

续表

序号	中文	英文
51	禁止向左转弯	No Left Turn
52	禁止运输危险物品车辆驶入	Vehicles Carrying Hazardous Materials Prohibited
53	禁止直行	No Straight Through
54	救援电话	First Aid Call
55	开车时禁止手持手机	Do Not Use Mobile Phone While Driving
56	靠左侧道路行驶	Keep Left
57	快速公交系统专用车道	Bus Rapid Transit Lane 或 BRT Lane 或 BRT Only〔用于 Lane 可省略的场合〕
58	连续弯路	Winding Road Ahead 或 Curves Ahead
59	连续下坡	Long Descent
60	两侧变窄	Road Narrows on Both Sides
61	两侧通行	Pass on Either Side
62	路面不平	Rough Road Ahead
63	路面低洼	Low-Lying Road Ahead
64	路面高突	Bumpy Road Ahead
65	慢行	Slow Down
66	免费通行	Toll Free

续表

序号	中文	英文
67	平稳驾驶	Drive Safely
68	前方 ____ 米进入无路灯路段	No Road Lights ____ Meters Ahead
69	前方桥低	Low Bridge Ahead
70	前方施工	Road Work Ahead
71	前方弯道	Bend Ahead
72	前方弯路慢行	Bend Ahead // Slow Down
73	前方学校，减速慢行	School Ahead // Slow Down
74	前方拥堵	Congestion Ahead
75	前方左急转弯	Sharp Left Turn Ahead
76	前方左侧绕行	Detour Ahead Left 或 Detour Left
77	前方左右绕行	Detour Ahead Left or Right
78	人行道封闭	Sidewalk Closed
79	施工	Road Work
80	施工请绕行	Construction Ahead // Detour
81	市区（指示市区方向）	To City 或 To Downtown
82	事故易发路段	CAUTION // Accident Black Spot

续表

序号	中文	英文
83	双向交通	Two-Way Traffic
84	隧道开车灯	Turn on Headlights Before Entering Tunnel
85	停车检查	Stop for Inspection
86	停车领卡	Stop for Toll Card
87	停车让行	STOP
88	危险路段	Dangerous Area
89	无路灯路段全长 ____ 米	No Road Lights Next ____ m
90	限制高度：____ 米	Maximum Clearance: ____ m
91	限制宽度：____ 米	Maximum Width: ____ m
92	限制速度：____ 千米 / 小时	Speed Limit: ____ km/h
93	限制重量：____ 吨	Weight Limit: ____ t
94	限制轴重：____ 吨	Axle Weight Limit: ____ t
95	向前 ____ 米	____ Meters Ahead
96	向左急转弯路	Sharp Curve to Left
97	向左转弯	Turn Left
98	小心滑坡	Landslide Hazard Area

续表

序号	中文	英文
99	小心雪天路滑	Road May Be Icy
100	学校附近禁止鸣笛	School Area // No Honking 或 No Horns
101	易滑	CAUTION // Slippery Surface
102	雨雪天气请慢行	Drive Slowly in Rain or Snow
103	直行	Go Straight
104	直行车道	Straight Lane〔Lane 可省略〕
105	注意保持车距	Keep Distance
106	注意避让学生，请减速慢行	SLOW // Student Crossing
107	注意非机动车	Watch for Non-Motor Vehicles
108	注意野生动物	Watch for Wild Animals
109	注意合流	Roads Merge 或 Lanes Merge
110	注意横风	Beware of Crosswind
111	注意火车	Beware of Trains
112	注意路面结冰	CAUTION // Icy Road
113	注意落石	DANGER // Falling Rocks
114	注意前方人行横道	Pedestrian Crossing Ahead

续表

序号	中文	英文
115	注意雾天	Drive Carefully in Foggy Weather
116	注意信号灯	Traffic Lights Ahead
117	注意雨雪天气	Drive Carefully in Rain or Snow
118	注意障碍物	Watch Out for Obstacles 或 CAUTION // Obstacles Ahead
119	转弯慢行	Turn Ahead // Slow Down
120	最低限速：____ 千米 / 小时	Minimum Speed: ____ km/h
121	左侧变窄	Road Narrows on Left
122	左转车道	Left-Turn Lane〔Lane 可省略〕

4. 南京市重要交通枢纽

序号	中文	英文
1	南京港	Nanjing Port
2	南京禄口国际机场	Nanjing Lukou International Airport
3	南京汽车客运南站	Nanjing South Coach Station
4	铁路南京南站	Nanjing South Railway Station 或 Nanjingnan Railway Station

续表

序号	中文	英文
5	铁路南京站	Nanjing Railway Station

三、商业服务

Part 3 Commercial services

1. 范围

本部分规定了南京市商业领域英文译写的相关术语和定义、译写要求和方法等。

本部分适用于南京市商业经营机构及服务信息、商业金融类机构及服务信息的英文译写。

2. 规范性引用文件

应用本部分内容需参考如下文件。如文件注明日期，则仅注日期的版本适用于本文件。如文件未注日期，则其最新版本（包括所有的修改单）适用于本部分。

汉语拼音方案（1958 年中华人民共和国第一届全国人民代表大会第五次会议审议通过）

GB 17733 地名 标志

GB/T 10001（所有部分）标志用公共信息图形符号

GB/T 16159 汉语拼音正词法基本规则

GB/T 30240.1—2013 公共服务领域英文译写规范（第 1 部分：通则）

GB/T 30240.9—2017 公共服务领域英文译写规范（第 9 部分：餐饮住宿）

GB/T 30240.10—2017 公共服务领域英文译写规范（第 10 部分：商业金融）

DB32/T 1446.6—2009 公共场所英文译写规范（第 6 部分：金融）

DB32/T 1446.8—2009 公共场所英文译写规范（第 8 部分：商业服务）

3. 术语和定义

下列术语和定义适用于本部分。

3.1 商业 commerce

从事商品（包括实物商品和服务商品）销售的行业。

3.2 餐饮业 catering

向消费者提供餐饮及相关服务的食品生产经营行业。

3.3 住宿业 accommodation

向消费者提供住宿及相关服务的行业。

3.4 金融业 finance

从事货币存取和信贷、货币流通、证券和期货交易、保险业务等活动的行业。

4. 译写要求

4.1 商业领域公共场所中文标识在 GB/T 10001.1 中已经规定了相应的图形符号时，应首先按照标准的规定使用公共信息图形符号。使用国际通用标识符号或图标的，可不提供英文译写。

4.2 商业领域公共场所中文标识采用英文译写时，英文单词的大小写应符合本指南第 1 部分的规定；采用汉语拼音标注时，拼写应符合 GB/T 16159 的规定。

5. 译写方法

5.1 商业、餐饮业、住宿业、金融业机构和场所名称

5.1.1 主要功能为购物、餐饮和商业活动的大型场所或大楼、大厦译作 Plaza。

集购物、休闲、娱乐、餐饮等于一体，包括百货店、大卖场以及众多专业连锁零售店在内的购物中心译作 Shopping Mall 或 Shopping Center。

5.1.2 只针对货品进行分类销售、不具有休闲娱乐等多种功能的较小规模的商店、店铺译作 Store 或 Shop。除了理发店 Barber Shop 等习惯用法或固定搭配外，通常情况下 Store 和 Shop 可以互换使用。专卖店采用“品牌名 +Store”或“品牌名 +Shop”的体例译写，Store 或 Shop 也可省略。

5.1.3 酒家、酒楼、酒店、菜馆、餐馆、餐厅、饭庄、食府以及饮食店等仅提供餐饮服务的服务机构，一般译作 Restaurant。中文名称中含有“阁、轩、府、坊、村、廊”等的，视作专名的一部分，连同专名一起用汉语拼音拼写，如：“奇芳阁” Qifangge Restaurant。

5.1.4 咖啡馆一般译作 Café，酒吧译作 Bar，茶馆译作 Teahouse。

5.1.5 宾馆以及提供住宿的酒店、饭店等译作 Hotel；经济型的连锁旅馆可译作 Inn。

5.1.6 银行译作 Bank，如：“南京银行” Bank of Nanjing。各银行在南京的分行均译作 Nanjing Branch，置于所属总行译名之后，如：“中国光大银行南京分行” China Everbright Bank Nanjing Branch。支行译作 Sub-Branch，可置于所属总行、分行译名之后，用逗号隔开，如：“交通银行南京分行新街口支行” Bank of Communications Nanjing Branch, Xinjiekou Sub-Branch。若“分行”

一词在中文名称中省略了，则可将分行与支行名称并列译出，如："中国银行南京江宁支行" Bank of China, Nanjing Jiangning Sub-Branch。银行的营业部译作 Banking Center 或 Banking Department，分理处译作 Office，储蓄所译作 Savings Agency。

5.1.7 股份有限公司、有限责任公司译作 Company Limited（可缩写为 Co., Ltd.），集团公司译作 Group，控股公司译作 Holdings Company 或 Holdings Co., Ltd.。保险、证券、期货、财务管理与服务类的公司译作 Company 或 Corporation, Company 和 Corporation 两者意义基本相同，具体根据"约定俗成"的原则选择使用。交易所译作 Exchange，证券交易所译作 Stock Exchange，期货交易所译作 Futures Exchange，证券公司译作 Securities，如："南京证券" Nanjing Securities。保险公司译作 Insurance Limited Company。

5.1.8 其他商业、金融业机构和场所名称的译写应符合 GB/T 30240.1—2013 中第 5.1 条的各项要求。

5.2 中餐菜肴名称

5.2.1 中餐菜肴的翻译需要考虑其主料（配料）和烹制方法，但是更重要的是简洁明快、易于上口，从而吸引顾客，推广中国餐饮文化。例如："葱油鸡"可以按"主料 + With/in + 配料 / 汤汁"的公式译作 Chicken With Scallion Oil，也可以直接译作 Scallion Oil Chicken。又如："红烧肉"可以按"做法（动词过去分词）+ 主料 + With/in + 配料 / 汤汁"的公式译作 Braised Pork in Brown Sauce，也可以直接译作 Braised Pork。具有中国特色的传统食品，可以使用汉语拼音，如："饺子" Jiaozi。

5.3 其他商业和金融服务信息的英文译写应符合 GB/T 30240.1—2013 和 GB/T 30240.10—2017 的规定。采用英文直接翻译时，应符合国际通用惯例。

商业服务英文译法示例

注：1. 以下词条在各自二级目录下按照汉语拼音字母的顺序排列（若词条以阿拉伯数字或英文字母开头，则置于表首。数字先排，从小到大；字母后排，按照字母表顺序）。

2. “〔 〕”中的内容是对英文译法的解释说明。“（ ）”及其所包含的内容如果是词条的组成部分应保留，如果是词条的缩写、简称或其它同义词语则可根据实际情况选择使用。

3. “／”表示“和”或者“或”，如果是词条的组成部分应保留，如果表示选择关系则根据情况选择使用。“//”表示换行。

1. 商业场所及服务信息

（1）商业场所和机构名称

序号	中文	英文
1	搬家公司	Moving Company
2	保洁公司	Cleaning Company
3	本地土特产店	Local Specialty Store
4	步行街	Pedestrian Street
5	仓储式会员店	Warehouse Membership Store
6	超市	Supermarket

续表

序号	中文	英文
7	成人用品商店	Adult Store
8	宠物商店	Pet Shop
9	宠物医院	Veterinary Hospital 或 Vet
10	电器城；家电城	Electronics and Home Appliances
11	儿童摄影室	Children's Photo Studio
12	发型工作室	Hair Studio
13	房产中介；房地产经纪公司	Real Estate Agency
14	分店	Branch Store
15	工艺品商店	Arts and Crafts Store
16	购物广场	Shopping Plaza
17	购物中心；百货商场	Shopping Mall 或 Shopping Center
18	花店	Florist's
19	婚庆公司	Wedding Services Company
20	婚纱影楼；婚纱摄影室	Wedding Photo Studio
21	家居建材商店	Home Furnishing & Building Material Store
22	家政服务公司	Domestic Services Company

续表

序号	中文	英文
23	金店	Gold Store
24	精品店	Boutique
25	理发店	Barber Shop
26	贸易中心	Trade Center
27	美发沙龙	Hair Dressing Salon
28	美容美体中心	Beauty and Body Care Center
29	免税店	Duty-Free Store
30	女子美容工作室	Ladies' Beauty Studio
31	商店	Store 或 Shop
32	商业街	Commercial Street
33	食品超市	Food Supermarket
34	市区购物中心	Urban Shopping Center
35	数码店	Electronics Store
36	数码工作室	Digital Studio
37	特卖场	Special Sales
38	体验馆	Exploration Hall 或 Discovery Hall

续表

序号	中文	英文
39	温泉会所	Hot Spring Club
40	物流公司	Logistics Company〔Company 可省略〕
41	物业公司	Property Management Company
42	洗浴中心	Bath Center
43	线上店	Online Store
44	形象设计中心	Image Design Center
45	眼镜店	Optical Shop
46	养生馆	Health Club
47	药店	Pharmacy
48	音像制品店	Audio-Video Store
49	照相馆；摄影室	Photo Studio
50	折扣店	Discount Store 或 Outlets
51	中央商务区	Central Business District
52	专卖店	Brand Store
53	装潢公司；装修公司	Interior Decoration Company
54	总店	Main Store

续表

序号	中文	英文
55	租车公司	Car Rental Company
56	租赁公司	Leasing Company
57	足疗店；足浴店	Foot Massage Shop

(2)商业设施及服务项目名称

序号	中文	英文
1	保温袋	Thermal Bag
2	裁剪熨烫	Tailoring and Ironing
3	超市出口	EXIT 或 Exit
4	超市入口	ENTRANCE 或 Entrance
5	宠物美容	Pet Grooming
6	改衣服务	Clothing Alteration Service
7	干洗	Dry Cleaning
8	公平秤	Check Scale
9	购物车	Shopping Cart

续表

序号	中文	英文
10	购物车回收处	Shopping Cart Return
11	购物筐	Shopping Basket
12	过磅处；称重处	Weigh Counter
13	环保袋	Environment-Friendly Bag
14	开发票处	Invoice and Receipt Issuance
15	裤边修改	Hemming Service
16	快照服务	Instant Photo Service
17	礼品包装	Gift Wrapping
18	美甲	Manicure
19	密封盒	Airtight Box
20	皮鞋修复和保养	Shoe Repair and Polish
21	商品保养及维修	Maintenance and Repair
22	商品邮寄及托运	Mailing and Delivery
23	试衣间	Fitting Room
24	手机充电处	Mobile Phone Recharging
25	首饰加工	Jewelry Smithing

续表

序号	中文	英文
26	送货服务	Delivery Service
27	饮水处	Drinking Water
28	照片冲印	Photo Processing
29	钟表维修	Watch and Clock Repair
30	自助收银区	Self Checkout

（3）商品种类名称

序号	中文	英文
1	办公用品	Office Supplies
2	保健食品	Health Food
3	保健用品	Healthcare Products
4	保暖内衣	Thermal Underwear
5	饼干	Biscuits
6	布艺	Fabrics and Lace
7	彩妆	Make-Up

续表

序号	中文	英文
8	衬衫	Shirts
9	冲饮	Instant Drinks
10	宠物用品	Pet Supplies
11	垂钓用具	Fishing Gear
12	淡水鱼	Freshwater Fish
13	电脑及配套设备	Computers and Accessories
14	豆制品	Bean Products
15	儿童服装	Children's Wear
16	儿童玩具	Children's Toys
17	儿童用品	Children's Products
18	耳钉	Ear Studs
19	耳环	Earrings
20	方便食品	Instant Food
21	翡翠饰品	Jade Accessories
22	蜂蜜	Honey
23	服装饰品	Clothing and Accessories

续表

序号	中文	英文
24	副食	Non-Staple Food
25	干海产品	Dried Seafood
26	干货	Dried Foods
27	干鲜果品	Dried and Fresh Fruits
28	干鲜蔬菜	Dried and Fresh Vegetables
29	工具书	Reference Books
30	罐头	Canned Food
31	果干；果脯；蜜饯	Dried Fruits
32	海鱼	Sea Fish
33	户外运动系列	Outdoor Sports Series
34	护发用品	Conditioner
35	护肤用品	Skin Care Products
36	化妆品	Cosmetics
37	家居用品	Household Supplies
38	家具	Furniture
39	家用电器	Household Appliances

续表

序号	中文	英文
40	健康食品	Healthy Food
41	健身器械	Fitness Equipment
42	戒指	Rings
43	进口商品	Imported Products
44	精品男装	Designer Men's Wear
45	精品女装	Designer Women's Wear
46	咖啡	Coffee
47	可穿戴科技产品	Wearable Technology Products
48	口腔清洁用品	Oral Hygiene Products
49	腊肉酱菜	Preserved Meat and Pickled Vegetables
50	乐器	Musical Instruments
51	领带	Ties
52	旅行箱包	Bags and Suitcases
53	毛织品	Woolens
54	面包	Bread
55	面包糕点	Bakery 或 Bread, Cakes and Pastries

续表

序号	中文	英文
56	名烟名酒	Brand Name Tobacco and Liquor
57	沐浴露	Shower Gel
58	奶粉	Powdered Milk
59	男裤	Men's Trousers
60	男配饰	Men's Accessories
61	男士服装	Men's Wear
62	男士休闲装	Men's Casual Wear
63	男士正装；男士西装；绅士正装	Men's Suits
64	男鞋	Men's Shoes
65	内衣	Underwear
66	女裤	Women's Trousers
67	女配饰；女士饰品	Women's Accessories
68	女士服装	Women's Wear 或 Ladies' Wear
69	女士内衣	Lingerie
70	女士休闲装	Women's Casual Wear
71	女鞋	Women's Shoes

续表

序号	中文	英文
72	皮具	Leatherware
73	啤酒	Beer
74	汽车用品	Car Accessories
75	巧克力；巧克力糖	Chocolate
76	曲奇	Cookies
77	日用百货	Household Necessities
78	日用品	Daily Necessities
79	散装食品	Bulk Food
80	商务休闲装	Business Casual Wear
81	手包；手袋	Handbags
82	手表	Watches
83	手机	Mobile Phones
84	手机配件	Mobile Phone Accessories
85	手机维修	Mobile Phone Repair
86	手链	Bracelets
87	蔬菜	Vegetables

续表

序号	中文	英文
88	熟食	Delicatessen〔也可简作 Deli〕或 Cooked Food
89	数码产品	Digital Products
90	水果	Fruits
91	速冻食品	Frozen Food
92	特价服装	Discount Clothes
93	特色食品	Specialty Food
94	体育用品	Sports Products
95	糖果	Candies
96	调料	Seasonings
97	通信器材	Communication Equipment
98	童袜	Children's Socks
99	童鞋	Children's Shoes
100	卫生用品	Sanitation Supplies
101	文化用品；学习用具	Stationery
102	五金灯具	Hardware and Lighting Products
103	洗涤用品	Detergent

续表

序号	中文	英文
104	洗发用品	Shampoo
105	洗手液	Liquid Hand Soap
106	鲜奶	Milk
107	鲜肉水产	Meat, Poultry and Aquatic Food
108	咸饼干	Crackers
109	咸货；腌制品	Salted Food
110	香水	Perfume
111	香皂	Soap
112	箱包	Bags and Suitcases
113	项链	Necklaces
114	项坠	Pendants
115	鞋帽	Shoes and Hats
116	休闲包	Casual Bags
117	休闲服装	Casual Wear
118	休闲食品	Snacks
119	烟机灶具	Range Hoods and Cooking Stoves

续表

序号	中文	英文
120	眼镜	Glasses
121	羊绒羊毛	Cashmere and Woolens
122	医疗器械	Medical Equipment
123	音像	Audio and Video Products
124	银饰品	Silver Accessories
125	婴儿食品	Baby Food
126	婴儿用品	Baby Products
127	泳装	Swimwear
128	羽绒服	Down Jackets
129	浴盐	Bath Salt
130	预制菜	Pre-Made Food
131	运动服装	Sportswear
132	运动器械；体育器材	Sports Equipment
133	运动鞋	Sports Shoes
134	运动休闲	Sports & Casual Wear
135	杂粮	Coarse Grains

续表

序号	中文	英文
136	针棉内衣	Knitted and Cotton Underwear
137	珍珠饰品	Pearl Accessories
138	职业男装	Men’s Suits
139	职业女装	Women’s Suits
140	纸制品	Paper Products
141	智能设备	Smart Devices
142	珠宝	Jewelry
143	钻石饰品	Diamond Accessories
144	电脑类（书籍）	Computer
145	法律类（书籍）	Law
146	工程类（书籍）	Engineering
147	工商类（书籍）	Business Administration
148	教辅（书籍）	Education
149	经济类（书籍）	Economics
150	科学类（书籍）	Science
151	其他（书籍）	Miscellaneous

续表

序号	中文	英文
152	实业类（书籍）	Industry
153	外文类（书籍）	Foreign Languages and Literature
154	文学类（书籍）	Literature
155	学术类（书籍）	Academic Books
156	艺术类（书籍）	Arts

（4）商业部门名称

序号	中文	英文
1	IT 部	IT Department
2	安全保卫部	Security Department
3	财务部	Finance Department
4	采购部	Purchasing Department
5	会计办公室	Accountant's Office
6	经理办公室	Manager's Office
7	客户服务部	Customer Service Department

续表

序号	中文	英文
8	人力资源部	Human Resources Department
9	市场部	Marketing Department
10	物流部	Logistics Department
11	物业行政部	Property and Administration Department
12	信息管理部	Information Management Department
13	运营保障部	Business Supporting Department
14	总经理办公室	General Manager's Office

（5）商业从业人员名称

序号	中文	英文
1	保洁员	Cleaner
2	策划师	Planner
3	产品经理	Product Manager
4	导购员	Shopping Guide
5	导游	Tour Guide

续表

序号	中文	英文
6	公关经理	Public Relations (PR) Manager
7	化妆师	Makeup Artist
8	咖啡师	Barista
9	快递员	Express Deliverer
10	买手	Buyer
11	美发师	Hair Stylist
12	美容师	Beautician
13	美妆博主	Beauty Blogger
14	模特	Model
15	人力资源总监	Chief Human Resources Officer (CHRO)
16	设计师	Designer
17	摄影师	Photographer
18	首席财务官	Chief Financial Officer (CFO)
19	首席采购官	Chief Procurement Officer (CPO)
20	首席技术官 / 技术总监	Chief Technology Officer (CTO)
21	首席内容官	Chief Content Officer (CCO)

续表

序号	中文	英文
22	首席体验官	Chief Experience Officer (CXO)
23	首席信息官	Chief Information Officer (CIO)
24	首席营销官	Chief Marketing Officer (CMO)
25	首席运营官	Chief Operating Officer (COO)
26	首席执行官	Chief Executive Officer (CEO)
27	调酒师	Bartender
28	外卖骑手	Delivery Rider
29	网络主播	Live Streamer
30	心理咨询师	Psychological Consultant
31	验光师	Optometrist
32	营养师	Nutritionist
33	营业员	Sales Assistant
34	主持人	Host

2. 餐饮业场所及服务信息

(1)餐饮业场所和机构名称

序号	中文	英文
1	便利店	Convenience Store
2	餐厅	Restaurant
3	茶馆	Teahouse
4	风味小吃	Local Snacks 或 Local Delicacies 或 Local Food
5	港式茶餐厅	Hong Kong-Style Restaurant〔规模较大〕或 Café 或 Diner〔规模较小〕
6	火锅店	Hot Pot Restaurant〔Restaurant 可省略〕
7	酒吧	Bar
8	咖啡馆	Café
9	烤鸭店	Roast Duck Restaurant
10	快餐店	Snack Bar 或 Fast Food Restaurant〔Restaurant 可省略〕
11	连锁快餐店	Fast Food Chain
12	美食广场	Food Plaza
13	美食街	Food Street
14	美食天地	Food Court

续表

序号	中文	英文
15	面包房	Bakery
16	面馆	Noodle Restaurant 或 Noodles〔用于 Restaurant 省略时〕
17	清真餐厅	Halal Restaurant
18	烧烤店	Grill House 或 Barbecue Restaurant〔Restaurant 可省略〕
19	食品杂货店	Grocery
20	素食餐厅	Vegetarian Restaurant
21	特色餐馆	Specialty Restaurant
22	西饼店	Pastry Store
23	西餐厅	Western Restaurant
24	小吃店	Snack Bar
25	中餐厅	Chinese Restaurant

（2）菜单及中西菜肴名称

序号	中文	英文
1	T 骨牛排	T-Bone Steak

续表

序号	中文	英文
2	扒菲力牛排	Grilled Fillet Steak
3	扒三文鱼排	Grilled Salmon Fillet
4	白斩鸡	Poached Chicken
5	包子	Baozi 或 Steamed Buns
6	北京烤鸭	Beijing Roast Duck
7	冰淇淋	Ice Cream
8	菜包	Vegetable Buns
9	菜单	Menu
10	餐前包	Bread
11	草莓慕斯	Strawberry Mousse
12	肠粉	Steamed Rice Rolls
13	炒米粉	Stir-Fried Rice Noodles
14	炒年糕	Stir-Fried Rice Cake
15	葱爆羊肉	Stir-Fried Scallion Lamb
16	葱油鸡	Scallion Oil Chicken
17	打卤面	Gravy Noodles

续表

序号	中文	英文
18	蛋炒饭	Fried Rice With Eggs
19	德国猪肘	Eisbein 或 German Pork Knuckle
20	东坡肉	Braised Dongpo Pork
21	法式焗蜗牛	French Style Baked Snails
22	法式苹果塔	French Apple Tart
23	法式香煎鹅肝	French Fried Foie Gras
24	菲力牛排	Fillet Steak
25	粉蒸排骨	Steamed Rice Coated Ribs
26	佛跳墙	Fotiaoqiang 或 Abalone Casserole
27	夫妻肺片	Beef Slices in Chili Sauce
28	副菜	Side Dishes
29	盖浇饭	Rice Topped With Meat & Vegetables
30	干式熟成	Dry-Aged
31	桂花糯米藕	Lotus Root Stuffed With Sticky Rice
32	和牛汉堡	Wagyu Burger
33	黑森林蛋糕	Black Forest Cake

续表

序号	中文	英文
34	黑松露奶油意式炖饭	Black Truffle Cream Risotto
35	红酒烩鹅肝	Braised Foie Gras in Red Wine
36	红烧鲫鱼	Braised Crucian Carp
37	红烧肉	Braised Pork
38	红烧羊肉	Braised Lamb
39	花卷	Huajuan 或 Steamed Rolls
40	回锅肉	Twice-Cooked Pork
41	惠灵顿牛排	Beef Wellington
42	馄饨（汤）	Wonton Soup
43	煎饼	Fried Pancake
44	煎羊排	Pan-Fried Lamb Ribs
45	酱香猪蹄	Pig Feet in Brown Sauce
46	金陵汤包	Meat Soup Buns
47	酒水单	Beverage and Wine List
48	菊叶蛋汤	Egg Drop Soup With Chrysanthemum Leaves
49	卡布奇诺	Cappuccino

续表

序号	中文	英文
50	凯撒沙拉	Caesar Salad
51	烤羊排	Baked Lamb Ribs
52	烤羊肉串	Lamb Kebabs
53	烤猪排	Baked Pork Ribs
54	辣白菜 / 泡菜	Kimchi
55	辣子鸡丁	Spicy Diced Chicken
56	凉拌面	Cold Noodles in Sauce
57	芦蒿炒香干	Mugwort With Dried Bean Curd
58	卤水拼盘	Assorted Marinated Meat
59	罗宋汤	Borscht
60	绿茶布丁	Green Tea Pudding
61	馒头	Mantou 或 Steamed Buns
62	美式咖啡	Americano
63	米粉；米线	Rice Noodles
64	面疙瘩	Dough Drop Soup
65	面条	Noodles

续表

序号	中文	英文
66	摩卡	Mocha
67	拿铁	Latte
68	奶油蘑菇汤	Greamy Mushroom Soup
69	泡椒凤爪	Pickled Chicken Feet
70	皮蛋瘦肉粥	Congee With Century Eggs
71	荠菜豆腐羹	Shepherds Purse and Tofu Soup
72	千层饼	Thousand-Layer Pancake
73	前菜	Starter
74	肉包	Meat Buns
75	肉眼牛排	Ribeye Steak
76	三杯鸡	Three-Cup Chicken 或 Stewed Chicken With Ginger and Wine in Casserole
77	三文鱼沙拉	Salmon Salad
78	上脑牛排	Chuck Roll Steak
79	烧饼	Sesame Pastry
80	烧鸡	Roast Chicken
81	烧卖	Shaomai 或 Steamed Rice Dumplings

续表

序号	中文	英文
82	蔬菜火腿沙拉	Vegetable Salad With Ham
83	涮羊肉	Instant-Boiled Mutton 或 Lamb Hot Pot
84	松鼠桂鱼	Sweet and Sour Mandarin Fish
85	素食菜单	Vegetarian Menu
86	汤	Soup
87	汤圆	Tangyuan 或 Sticky Rice Balls
88	汤面	Noodle Soup
89	糖醋鱼	Sweet and Sour Fish
90	套餐菜单	Set Menu
91	提拉米苏	Tiramisu
92	甜品	Dessert
93	甜品单	Dessert Menu
94	土豆沙拉	Potato Salad
95	西红柿炒鸡蛋	Scrambled Eggs With Tomatoes
96	西冷牛排	Sirloin Steak
97	虾饺	Steamed Shrimp Dumplings

续表

序号	中文	英文
98	虾仁豆腐	Tofu With Shrimp
99	虾仁馄饨（汤）	Shrimp Wonton Soup
100	鲜虾牛油果沙拉	Shrimp and Avocado Salad
101	馅饼	Meat Pie
102	香浓牛尾汤	Oxtail Soup
103	香酥鸡	Crispy Chicken
104	小姜饼	Gingerbread
105	蟹黄豆腐	Tofu With Crab Roe
106	盐水鸭	Salted Duck
107	意大利面	Spaghetti
108	鱼圆汤	Fish Ball Soup
109	炸春卷	Deep-Fried Spring Rolls
110	炸酱面	Noodles With Soybean Paste
111	战斧牛排	Tomahawk Steak
112	蒸糕	Steamed Cake
113	芝士蛋糕	Cheese Cake

续表

序号	中文	英文
114	粥	Rice Congee
115	猪肉馄饨（汤）	Pork Wonton Soup
116	猪肉水饺	Pork Dumplings
117	主菜	Main Course
118	主食	Staple Food
119	孜然羊肉	Stir-Fried Lamb With Cumin
120	粽子	Zongzi (Rice Dumplings Wrapped in Reed or Bamboo Leaves)

（3）酒水名称

序号	中文	英文
1	白酒	Chinese Baijiu 或 Chinese Liquor
2	白兰地	Brandy
3	百威啤酒	Budweiser
4	朝日啤酒	Asahi Beer
5	伏特加	Vodka

续表

序号	中文	英文
6	干白	Dry White Wine
7	干红	Dry Red Wine
8	国缘	Guoyuan Liquor
9	哈尔滨啤酒	Harbin Beer
10	嘉士伯啤酒	Carlsberg
11	金酒	Gin
12	朗姆酒	Rum
13	龙舌兰	Tequila
14	茅台	Moutai
15	梦之蓝	Dream Blue
16	葡萄酒	Wine
17	青岛啤酒	Tsingtao Beer
18	清酒	Sake
19	烧酒	Soju
20	威士忌	Whisky
21	五粮液	Wuliangye Liquor

续表

序号	中文	英文
22	喜力啤酒	Heineken
23	雪花啤酒	Snow Beer
24	燕京啤酒	Yanjing Beer
25	张裕香槟	Changyu Sparkling Cider

（4）调味品名称

序号	中文	英文
1	醋	Vinegar
2	番茄酱	Tomato Sauce 或 Ketchup
3	橄榄油	Olive Oil
4	果酱	Jam
5	胡椒粉	Pepper 或 Ground Pepper
6	花椒	Sichuan Pepper
7	黄油	Butter
8	酱油	Soy Sauce

续表

序号	中文	英文
9	椒盐粉	Peppered Salt
10	芥末酱	Mustard
11	辣椒酱	Chili Sauce
12	奶酪	Cheese
13	色拉酱	Salad Dressings
14	糖	Sugar
15	调味品（香辛料）	Condiments 或 Spices
16	盐	Salt
17	孜然粉	Cumin Powder

（5）餐具名称

序号	中文	英文
1	白酒杯	Shot Glass
2	白葡萄酒杯	White Wine Glass
3	杯垫	Coaster

续表

序号	中文	英文
4	杯碟	Saucer
5	冰夹	Ice Tongs
6	冰桶	Ice Bucket
7	餐巾；餐巾纸	Napkin
8	餐具	Tableware
9	叉	Fork
10	茶杯	Teacup
11	茶壶	Teapot
12	刀	Knife
13	碟	Plate
14	分酒器	Dispenser
15	公筷	Serving Chopsticks
16	红酒杯	Red Wine Glass
17	酒杯	Glass
18	筷子	Chopsticks
19	汤匙	Spoon

续表

序号	中文	英文
20	碗	Bowl
21	香槟杯	Champagne Glass
22	醒酒器	Decanter

（4）餐饮业从业人员名称

序号	中文	英文
1	餐厅服务员	Waiter〔无论男女〕或 Wait Staff
2	餐厅领位员	Receptionist
3	餐饮部经理	Food & Beverage Manager
4	厨工	Kitchen Helper
5	厨师	Cook
6	副厨师长	Sous Chef
7	行政主厨	Executive Chef
8	收银员；收款台；收银处	Cashier
9	西餐部经理	Western Restaurant Manager

续表

序号	中文	英文
10	洗碗工	Dish Washer
11	宴会部经理	Banquet Manager
12	中餐部经理	Chinese Restaurant Manager
13	主厨；厨师长	Head Chef

3. 酒店业场所及服务信息

（1）酒店业场所名称

序号	中文	英文
1	包间；包房	Private Room
2	标准间；标准客房	Standard Room
3	宾馆；酒店；旅馆；饭店	Hotel
4	长包房	Long Stay Room
5	大床房	King Size Room
6	大堂；大厅	Lobby
7	大堂经理台	Lobby Manager Desk〔Desk 可省略〕

续表

序号	中文	英文
8	单人间	Single Room
9	点菜区	Food Ordering Area
10	订餐处；预订处	Reservation
11	度假酒店	Resort Hotel
12	房间种类	Room Type
13	高级房	Superior Room
14	高级套房	Senior Suite
15	观光酒店；旅游饭店	Tourist Hotel
16	贵宾餐厅	VIP Dining Room
17	海景房	Sea View Room
18	行政办公室	Administration Office
19	行政房	Executive Room
20	行政酒廊	Executive Lounge
21	行政套房	Executive Suite
22	豪华房	Deluxe Room
23	豪华酒店	Deluxe Hotel

续表

序号	中文	英文
24	豪华套房	Deluxe Suite
25	候餐区	Waiting Area
26	家庭房	Family Room
27	经济型连锁旅馆	Inn
28	精品酒店	Boutique Hotel
29	酒店大堂	Hotel Lobby
30	客房	Guest Room
31	客房部	Housekeeping Department
32	快捷酒店	Budget Hotel
33	连锁酒店	Chain Hotel
34	美容院；美容护理部	Beauty Care
35	民宿	Homestay
36	普通套房	Junior Suite
37	前台；服务台；接待处	Front Desk 或 Reception
38	青年旅社	Youth Hostel
39	三人间	Triple Room

续表

序号	中文	英文
40	山景房	Hill View Room 或 Mountain View Room
41	商务房	Business Room
42	商务酒店	Business Hotel
43	双人间（两张单人床）	Twin Room
44	水疗美容部；水疗生活馆	Spa
45	套房	Suite
46	无烟房	Non-Smoking Room
47	无障碍客房	Accessible Room
48	西厨房	Western Kitchen
49	星级饭店	Star-Rated Hotel
50	宴会厅	Banquet Hall
51	园景房	Garden View Room
52	中厨房	Chinese Kitchen
53	主题酒店	Theme Hotel
54	自助餐厅	Buffet 或 Cafeteria
55	总服务台	Information and Reception Desk

续表

序号	中文	英文
56	总机房	Operator Room
57	总统套房	Presidential Suite

（2）酒店业用品及设施名称

序号	中文	英文
1	被套	Duvet Cover
2	被子	Comforter〔无被套〕或 Duvet〔有被套〕
3	擦鞋布	Shoe Shine Cloth
4	床单	Fitted Sheet
5	房卡	Room Card
6	行李车	Baggage Cart
7	行李房	Baggage Room
8	行李服务台	Baggage Counter
9	行李寄存牌	Baggage Tag
10	行李架	Baggage Stand

续表

序号	中文	英文
11	健身房	Fitness Room
12	俱乐部	Club
13	礼宾部	Concierge Office
14	毛巾	Towel
15	毛毯袋	Blanket Bag
16	棉签	Cotton Swab
17	润肤露	Lotion
18	手推车	Cart
19	毯子	Blanket
20	拖鞋	Slippers
21	卫生袋	Sanitary Bag
22	问讯处	Enquiry 或 Information
23	洗衣袋	Laundry Bag
24	洗衣单	Laundry Docket
25	牙膏	Toothpaste
26	牙刷	Toothbrush

续表

序号	中文	英文
27	牙线	Flosser 或 Floss
28	针线盒；针线包	Sewing Kit
29	枕头	Pillow

（3）酒店业从业人员名称

序号	中文	英文
1	采购部经理	Purchasing Manager
2	副总经理	Deputy General Manager
3	行李员	Porter
4	酒店修理工	Maintenance Worker
5	客房服务员	Room Attendant
6	客房清洁人员	Housekeeping Staff
7	客房主管	Housekeeping Supervisor
8	前厅经理	Front Office Manager
9	夜班经理	Night Shift Manager

续表

序号	中文	英文
10	预订部经理	Reservation Manager
11	预订及总机专员	Reservation and Operator Agent
12	值班经理	Duty Manager
13	总经理	General Manager

4. 金融业场所及服务信息

（1）金融业场所和机构名称

序号	中文	英文
1	24 小时自助银行	24-Hour Self-Service Banking
2	保险公司	Insurance Company
3	财产保险公司	Property Insurance Company
4	财务公司	Finance Company
5	城市商业银行	Urban Commercial Bank
6	典当行	Pawn Shop
7	分行	Branch

续表

序号	中文	英文
8	分理处	Office
9	华泰证券	Huatai Securities
10	货币经纪公司	Money Brokerage Company
11	金融资产管理公司	Asset Management Company
12	金融租赁公司	Financial Leasing Company
13	南京银行	Bank of Nanjing
14	南京证券	Nanjing Securities
15	农村商业银行	Rural Commercial Bank
16	拍卖公司	Auction Company
17	拍卖行	Auction House
18	期货公司	Futures Company
19	期货交易所	Futures Exchange
20	期货经纪公司	Futures Brokerage Company
21	人寿保险公司	Life Insurance Company
22	投资咨询公司	Investment Consulting Company
23	小额贷款公司	Micro-Loan Company

续表

序号	中文	英文
24	信托公司	Trust Company
25	银行	Bank
26	银行营业部	Banking Center 或 Banking Department
27	邮政储蓄银行	Postal Savings Bank
28	证券公司（股份有限公司、有限责任公司）	Securities Company Limited
29	证券交易所	Stock Exchange
30	证券投资基金管理公司	Securities Investment Fund Management Company
31	支行	Sub-Branch
32	紫金农商银行	Zijin Rural Commercial Bank

（2）金融业设施名称

序号	中文	英文
1	理财专区	Wealth Management Area
2	填单处	Form Filling Area
3	外币储蓄点	Foreign Currency Deposit Service

续表

序号	中文	英文
4	网银体验区	E-Banking Experience Area
5	现金服务区	Cash Service Area
6	业务柜台	Teller Counter
7	业务咨询处	Information
8	智能柜员机	Smart Teller Machine
9	咨询引导区	Consulting Area
10	自动存款机	Cash Deposit Machine
11	自动取款机	ATM
12	自助服务区	Self-Service Area
13	自助缴费机	Self-Service Payment Machine
14	自助取号机	Queue Ticket Dispenser

（3）金融业从业人员名称

序号	中文	英文
1	大堂经理	Lobby Manager
2	个人理财顾问	Personal Financial Advisor

续表

序号	中文	英文
3	柜员	Teller
4	理财经理	Financial Planning Manager
5	银行行长	Bank President

5. 商业服务信息提示

（1）餐饮业

序号	中文	英文
1	不可食用	Not Edible
2	餐具回收处	Leave Used Dishes Here
3	餐具已消毒	Sterilized
4	代客泊车	Valet Parking
5	光盘行动，不浪费	Clean Plates. No Waste.
6	广播服务	Broadcast Service
7	酒后代驾服务	Designated Driver Service
8	轮椅租用	Wheelchair Rental

续表

序号	中文	英文
9	旅客留言	Passengers' Messages
10	旅客投诉接待	Passenger Complaints
11	免费泊车	Free Parking
12	免费调料区	Free Seasonings
13	免费小菜	Free Appetizers
14	请依次取餐	Please Wait in Line
15	扫码点菜	Scan to Order
16	失物招领	Lost and Found
17	适量取食，请勿浪费	Take Only What You Need // Do Not Waste Food
18	提供轮椅	Wheelchairs Available
19	提供手杖	Walking Sticks Available
20	无障碍服务	Accessible Services
21	谢绝外带食物	Outside Food Not Allowed 或 No Outside Food
22	已预订；预留	Reserved
23	注意高温，当心烫伤	CAUTION // Hot Surface

（2）酒店业

序号	中文	英文
1	房价	Room Rate
2	访客请登记	All Visitors Must Register
3	加床	Cot 或 Extra Bed
4	仅对酒店客人开放	Hotel Guests Only
5	客房服务；送餐服务	Room Services
6	请打扫房间	Please Make up Room
7	请勿打扰	Please Do Not Disturb
8	入住登记	Check-in
9	提前抵达	Early Arrival
10	停车场仅对酒店客人开放	Parking for Hotel Guests Only
11	退房	Check-out
12	预抵日期	Expected Arrival Date
13	预付押金	Advance Deposit
14	预离日期	Expected Departure Date

（3）金融业

序号	中文	英文
1	（票据的）拒付 / 拒收 / 退票	Dishonor (of a Check)
2	本机每笔最大存款额：____ 元	Maximum ____ Yuan Deposit Each Time
3	出门请按钮	Press to Exit
4	磁卡插口	Card Slot
5	定期存款	Time Deposit
6	对公业务（企业银行服务）	Corporate Banking
7	对私业务（个人银行服务）	Personal Banking
8	挂失	Loss Reporting
9	挂失止付（汇票）	Loss Report and Stop-Payment
10	国际结算业务	International Settlement Business
11	国际业务	International Banking
12	汇兑	Exchange 或 Transfer
13	活期存款	Demand Deposit
14	活期存款账户	Current Account
15	活期存折	Savings Account Passbook

续表

序号	中文	英文
16	交通银行南京分行新街口支行	Bank of Communications Nanjing Branch, Xinjiekou Sub-Branch
17	节假日不办理（不营业）	Closed on Weekends and Public Holidays
18	节假日营业时间	Open Hours on Public Holiday
19	进门请刷卡	Swipe Card to Enter
20	跨行转账	Interbank Transfer
21	理财服务	Financial Planning Services
22	凭条口	Receipt
23	请排队等候叫号	Please Wait for Your Number to Be Called
24	请输入密码	Please Enter Your Password
25	如需帮助，请拨打总机	For Assistance, Please Call Operator
26	如需人工服务，请至 ____ 号窗口	Please Go to Window No. ____ for Staff Assistance
27	涉外服务	Foreign Services
28	市价交易	Market Price Transaction
29	收费项目	Pay Items
30	通知存款	Call Deposit
31	退汇	Refund

续表

序号	中文	英文
32	外币对公结算	Corporate Foreign Exchange Settlement
33	外汇查询	Foreign Exchange Inquiry
34	外汇兑换	Foreign Currency Exchange
35	外汇业务	Foreign Exchange Business
36	无卡存折	No-Card Deposit
37	现金业务	Cash Business
38	一卡通金卡业务	All-in-One Gold Card Services
39	营业时间：____ 点到 ____ 点	Open From ____ to ____
40	账单出口	Bill Out
41	账户余额查询	Balance Inquiry
42	中国光大银行南京分行	China Everbright Bank Nanjing Branch
43	中国银行南京江宁支行	Bank of China, Nanjing Jiangning Sub-Branch
44	自助服务终端	Self-Service Terminal

（4）通用类

序号	中文	英文
1	（全场）最低价	Best Prices
2	本商场设有闭路电视监控。	This Area Is Under Video Surveillance.
3	产地	Place of Origin
4	等级	Class 或 Grade
5	店庆促销	Anniversary Sale
6	服务承诺	Commitment to Our Customers
7	购物车仅限超市购物使用，请不要将购物车推出商场停车场以外。	Shopping Cart for Store Use Only. Please Leave it in Parking Lot. 或 Do Not Take Shopping Cart Beyond Parking Lot.
8	购物指南（导购图）	Shopping Directory
9	规格	Specifications
10	节日促销	Holiday Sale
11	零售	Retail
12	批发	Wholesale
13	品名	Product Name
14	全市范围免费送货	Free City-Wide Delivery
15	扫码支付	Scan to Pay

续表

序号	中文	英文
16	商场楼层平面图	Shopping Mall Floor Plan
17	试营业	Soft Opening
18	手语服务	Sign Language Services
19	售后服务热线	After-Sales Service Hotline
20	售完	Sold Out
21	条码扫描口	Barcode Scanner
22	团购服务	Group Purchase Services
23	退税	Tax Refund
24	消防疏散示意图	Fire Evacuation Chart
25	小心试穿，请勿污损衣物	Do Not Leave Any Stain on Clothes
26	易碎商品，小心轻放	Fragile! Handle With Care
27	预售	Advance Sale 或 Sale in Advance
28	____ 折（指优惠的折扣幅度）	____ Off〔九折为 10% Off，八折为 20% Off，以此类推〕
29	注意保护个人信息	Please Guard Your Personal Information

6. 新经济领域

序号	中文	英文
1	博主	Blogger
2	车载充电机	On-Board Charger
3	储能装置	Energy Storage
4	纯电动汽车	Battery Electric Vehicle (BEV)
5	点赞	Hit the Like 或 Thumbs-up
6	电动汽车	Electric Vehicle (EV)
7	电商直播	E-Commerce Live Streaming
8	粉丝经济	Fan Economy
9	共享经济	Sharing Economy
10	购买力	Purchasing Power
11	关注	Follow
12	光伏发电	Photovoltaic Power Generation
13	光学电子	Optical Electronics
14	混合动力电动汽车	Hybrid Electric Vehicle (HEV)
15	可再生能源	Renewable Energy Sources

续表

序号	中文	英文
16	跨境电商	Cross-Border E-Commerce
17	绿色电力	Green Power
18	能源数字化	Energy Digitization
19	氢能	Hydrogen Energy
20	区块链	Blockchain
21	驱动电机	Drive Motor
22	取关	Unfollow
23	圈粉	Attract Followers
24	人机交互	Human-Computer Interaction
25	社交媒体	Social Media
26	社交网络	Social Network
27	数字能源	Digital Energy
28	数字人民币	Digital RMB
29	太阳能	Solar Energy
30	太阳能电站	Solar Power Station
31	碳达峰	Carbon Peaking

续表

序号	中文	英文
32	碳中和	Carbon Neutrality
33	网红	Social Media Influencer
34	网红经济	Internet Celebrity Economy
35	网络平台	Online Platform
36	网上零售	Online Retail
37	未来网络	Future Internet
38	先进通信	Advanced Telecommunication
39	物联网	Internet of Things
40	限量发售	Limited Edition
41	新材料	New Material
42	新基建	New Infrastructure
43	新媒体	New Media
44	新型储能产业	New Energy-Storage Industry
45	元宇宙	Metaverse
46	云计算	Cloud Computing
47	在线直播	Streaming Online

续表

序号	中文	英文
48	直播	Live Stream
49	直播间	Live Room
50	直播经济	Live Streaming Economy
51	主播	Live Streamer

四、文化旅游

Part 4 Culture and tourism

1. 范围

本部分规定了南京市文化旅游服务领域英文译写的相关术语和定义、译写要求和方法等。

本部分适用于南京市文化旅游场所和机构名称、文化旅游服务信息的英文译写。

2. 规范性引用文件

应用本部分内容需参考如下文件。如文件注明日期，则仅注日期的版本适用于本文件。如文件未注日期，则其最新版本（包括所有的修改单）适用于本部分。

汉语拼音方案（1958 年中华人民共和国第一届全国人民代表大会第五次会议审议通过）

GB 17733 地名 标志

GB/T 10001（所有部分）标志用公共信息图形符号

GB/T 16159 汉语拼音正词法基本规则

GB/T 30240.1—2013 公共服务领域英文译写规范（第 1 部分：通则）

GB/T 30240.3—2017 公共服务领域英文译写规范（第 3 部分：旅游）

GB/T 30240.4—2017 公共服务领域英文译写规范（第 4 部分：文化娱乐）

DB32/T 1446.3—2009 公共场所英文译写规范（第 3 部分：旅游）

DB32/T 1446.4—2009 公共场所英文译写规范（第 4 部分：文化体育）

3. 术语和定义

下列术语和定义适用于本部分。

3.1　文化场馆 cultural venues

向公众开放，具有文化和艺术收藏、展示、传播、教育等功能的公益性场所。

注：文化场馆包括博物馆、美术馆、艺术馆、展览馆、纪念馆、科技馆、图书馆、档案馆、文史馆及旧址、故居等相关文化单位。

3.2　旅游景区景点 tourist areas and scenic spots

具有参观游览、休闲度假、康乐健身等功能，具备相应旅游服务设施并提供相应旅游服务，有统一的经营管理机构和明确的地域范围的独立管理区，包括风景区、旅游度假区、自然保护区、寺庙观堂、主题公园、森林公园、地质公园、游乐园、动物园、植物园，以及工业、农业、经贸、科教、军事、体育、文化艺术等各类旅游景区景点。

4. 译写要求

4.1　文化旅游领域公共场所中文标识在 GB/T 10001.1 中已经规定了相应的图形符号时，应首先按照标准的规定使用公共信息图形符号。使用国际通用标识符号或图标的，可不提供英文译写。

4.2　文化旅游领域公共场所中文标识采用英文译写时，英文单词的大小写应符合本指南第 1 部分的规定；采用汉语拼音标注时，拼写应符合 GB/T 16159 的规定。

5. 译写方法

5.1 文化场馆和相关机构名称

5.1.1 博物馆（院）译作 Museum，如：“南京博物院”Nanjing Museum。美术馆、艺术馆译作 Art Gallery 或 Art Museum，如：“金陵美术馆”Jinling Art Museum。具有展示、陈列功能的场馆译作 Exhibition Center 或 Exhibition Hall，如：“南京国际展览中心”Nanjing International Exhibition Center。

5.1.2 故居译作 Former Residence，如：“傅抱石故居”Former Residence of Fu Baoshi。

5.1.3 剧场、剧院、舞台、戏院、戏苑等均译作 Theater，音乐厅译作 Concert Hall，影院译作 Cinema，文化馆译作 Cultural Center。

5.1.4 其他文化场馆名称的译写应符合 GB/T 30240.1—2013 中第 5.1 条的各项要求。

5.2 旅游景区景点名称

5.2.1 山译作 Mountain 或 Hill，已经习惯使用 Mount 的可继续沿用，如：“钟山”Zhongshan Mountain。江、河译作 River，如：“秦淮河”Qinhuai River。湖译作 Lake，如：“玄武湖”Xuanwu Lake。

5.2.2 佛教的寺、庙译作 Temple，如：“栖霞寺”Qixia Temple。清真寺译作 Mosque，如：“草桥清真寺”Caoqiao Mosque，“净觉寺”Jingjue Mosque。教堂一般译作 Church，如：“南京圣保罗教堂”Nanjing St Paul's Church。

5.2.3 塔应区分不同的情况，采用不同的译法：佛塔译作 Pagoda，舍利塔译作 Stupa。其他的塔译作 Tower，如：“广播电视塔”Radio and TV Tower。

5.2.4　动物园译作 Zoo，如：“南京红山森林动物园” Nanjing Hongshan Forest Zoo。植物园译作 Botanical Garden，如：“南京中山植物园” Nanjing Zhongshan Botanical Garden。

5.2.5　亭、台、楼、阁、榭、阙等与专名一起使用汉语拼音拼写。根据对外服务的需要，可以后加英文予以解释，如：“湖心亭” Huxinting (Mid-Lake Pavilion)。

5.2.6　其他旅游景区景点名称的译写应符合 GB/T 30240.1—2013、GB/T 30240.3—2017 和 GB/T 30240.4—2017 的规定。

5.3　旅游服务信息

5.3.1　功能设施信息

5.3.1.1　以译出设施的功能信息为主。如：“团队通道” 可译作 Groups，“团队” 的功能须译出，“通道” 作为设施名称时可不译出。

5.3.1.2　标有阿拉伯数字的功能设施，采用“设施名 + 阿拉伯数字”的译写方法，如：“2 号看台” Platform 2。

5.3.1.3　其他旅游服务信息的译写应符合 GB/T 30240.1—2013 中第 5.2 条的各项要求。

5.3.2　警示警告信息

5.3.2.1　应明确具体事项，如：“儿童须有成人陪同” Children Must Be Accompanied by an Adult。

5.3.2.2　应明确所警示的对象主体。如：“外来车辆禁止入内” 译作 No Admittance to Outside Vehicles，不宜简单译作 No Admittance。

5.3.2.3　可以采用英文大写字母使指令更加醒目，如：“请勿触摸” NO TOUCHING，“未成年人禁止入内” CHILDREN NOT ALLOWED。

文化旅游英文译法示例

注：1. 以下词条在各自二级目录下按照汉语拼音字母的顺序排列（若词条以阿拉伯数字或英文字母开头，则置于表首。数字先排，从小到大；字母后排，按照字母表顺序）。

2. “〔 〕”中的内容是对英文译法的解释说明。“（ ）”及其所包含的内容如果是词条的组成部分应保留，如果是词条的缩写、简称或其它同义词语则可根据实际情况选择使用。

3. “／”表示“和”或者“或”，如果是词条的组成部分应保留，如果表示选择关系则根据情况选择使用。“//”表示换行。

1. 文化场馆名称

序号	中文	英文
1	博物馆	Museum
2	瓷器馆	Porcelain Gallery 或 Porcelains〔用于 Gallery 可省略的场合〕
3	大剧院	Grand Theater
4	大舞台	Grand Stage
5	道观	Daoist Temple
6	地质博物馆	Geological Museum
7	电影博物馆	Film Museum

续表

序号	中文	英文
8	动物园	Zoo
9	佛塔	Pagoda
10	歌剧院	Opera House
11	工艺美术馆	Arts and Crafts Museum
12	古代家具馆	Ancient Furniture Gallery〔Gallery 可省略〕
13	古代钱币馆	Ancient Coins Gallery〔Gallery 可省略〕
14	古代珍宝馆	Historical Treasures Gallery〔Gallery 可省略〕
15	故居	Former Residence
16	广播电视塔	Radio and TV Tower
17	航空博物馆	Aviation Museum
18	航天博物馆	Aerospace Museum
19	画廊	Gallery
20	活动中心	Activity Center
21	教堂	Church
22	剧院；剧场	Theater
23	烈士陵园	Martyrs' Cemetery

续表

序号	中文	英文
24	美术馆；艺术馆	Art Gallery
25	农业博物馆	Agricultural Museum
26	栖霞寺	Qixia Temple
27	漆器馆	Lacquer Gallery〔Gallery 可省略〕
28	青铜器馆	Bronze Gallery 或 Bronzes〔用于 Gallery 可省略的场合〕
29	清真寺	Mosque
30	舍利塔	Stupa
31	社区文化馆	Community Cultural Center
32	圣保罗教堂	St Paul’s Church
33	石刻艺术博物馆	Stone Carving Art Museum
34	书画馆；字画馆	Calligraphy and Paintings Gallery〔Gallery 可省略〕
35	体育博物馆	Sports Museum
36	文化陈列馆	Culture Exhibition Hall
37	现代书画馆	Modern Calligraphy and Paintings Gallery〔Gallery 可省略〕
38	演出社	Performing Arts Troupe
39	遗址博物馆	Historical Site Museum

续表

序号	中文	英文
40	艺术博物馆	Art Museum
41	艺术空间	Art Space
42	艺术文化中心	Art and Cultural Center
43	音乐厅	Concert Hall
44	影城	Cineplex 或 Cinema
45	油画馆	Oil Paintings Gallery〔Gallery 可省略〕
46	玉器馆	Jade Gallery〔Gallery 可省略〕
47	展馆	Exhibition Hall 或 Exhibition Gallery〔后者用于美术馆〕
48	植物园	Botanical Garden
49	中国画馆	Chinese Paintings Gallery
50	自然博物馆	Natural History Museum

2. 文化场馆设施及服务信息

序号	中文	英文
1	（舞台）后台	Backstage

续表

序号	中文	英文
2	____ 排	Row ____
3	____ 座	Seat ____
4	标本室	Specimen Room〔Room 可省略〕
5	触摸区	Hands-on Area 或 Touch Area
6	导览机	Audio Guide
7	灯光控制室	Lighting Control Room
8	动手项目；动手操作	Hands-on Activities
9	多媒体导览	Multimedia Guide
10	复刻品	Replica
11	观众通道	Audience Passage〔Passage 可省略〕
12	馆藏（指文物）	Museum Collection
13	贵宾间	VIP Box
14	化妆间	Dressing Room
15	会议展览中心	Convention and Exhibition Center
16	讲解服务；导游服务	Guide Services
17	礼品店	Gift Store 或 Gift Shop

续表

序号	中文	英文
18	民间收藏（指文物）	Private Collection
19	排练厅	Rehearsal Room
20	青铜器	Bronzeware
21	入口厅	Entrance Hall
22	视频转播室	Video Control Room
23	视听室	Audio-Visual Room
24	团体接待	Group Reception
25	文创伴手礼	Cultural and Creative Souvenirs
26	文物鉴定（多为古董）	Antique Authentication 或 Antique Appraisals
27	谢幕	Curtain Call
28	巡回展览	Itinerant Exhibition 或 Roving Exhibition
29	演播厅	Studio
30	演员休息室	Green Room
31	演职人员通道；演员专用通道	Performers Passage 或 Performers Only〔用于 Passage 可省略的场合〕
32	音响控制室	Sound Control Room
33	玉器	Jadeware

续表

序号	中文	英文
34	展板	Display Board 或 Display Panel
35	展场；展区	Exhibition Area
36	展柜	Showcase
37	展架	Display Rack
38	展品	Exhibits
39	展室	Exhibition Room
40	展厅	Exhibition Hall
41	展位	Booth
42	主题展览	Theme Exhibition
43	综合性展览	General Exhibition 或 Comprehensive Exhibition

3. 旅游设施及服务信息

序号	中文	英文
1	____ 米以下儿童免票	Free for Children Under ____ Meter(s)
2	3A 级旅游景区	National 3A-Level Scenic Area 或 3A Scenic Area

续表

序号	中文	英文
3	4A 级旅游景区	National 4A-Level Scenic Area 或 4A Scenic Area
4	5A 级旅游景区	National 5A-Level Scenic Area 或 5A Scenic Area
5	摆渡车落客区	Shuttle Bus Drop-Off
6	摆渡车停靠点	Shuttle Bus Terminal
7	冰雪活动	Winter Sports
8	茶室	Teahouse
9	禅修体验区	Meditation Area
10	成人票：____ 元	Adult: ____ Yuan
11	出口方向	Way Out
12	垂钓区	Angling Area
13	当日使用，逾期作废	Valid Only on Day of Issue〔指购票当日有效〕; Valid Only for the Date on Ticket〔指票面印刷的日期当日有效〕
14	登山避险处	Mountain Refuge
15	儿童票：____ 元	Child: ____ Yuan
16	儿童浅水活动区	Children's Wading Pool
17	服装租用	Costume Rental

续表

序号	中文	英文
18	抚摸区（可抚摸动物）	Petting Area
19	观光车	Sightseeing Bus
20	观光船；游船	Sightseeing Boat
21	观光廊	Sightseeing Corridor
22	观光索道	Sightseeing Cableway
23	观光线路	Sightseeing Route
24	观光小火车	Sightseeing Train
25	观景台	Observation Platform 或 Viewing Platform
26	观鸟区；鸟类观赏区	Bird-Watching Area
27	观赏区	Viewing Area
28	管理处	Management Office
29	广播室；广播站	Broadcasting Room
30	过山车	Roller Coaster
31	海滨浴场	Bathing Beach
32	滑冰	Skating
33	滑草	Grass Skiing

续表

序号	中文	英文
34	滑道戏水	Water Sliding
35	滑雪	Skiing
36	急救箱	First Aid Kit
37	健身步道	Fitness Trail
38	景区一日游	Day Tour
39	救生圈	Life Ring
40	卡丁车	Go-Kart 或 Go-Karting
41	缆车；索道缆车；空中缆车	Cable Car
42	缆车售票处	Cableway Ticket Office
43	临时出口	Temporary Exit
44	露营地	Camping Area
45	轮椅租借	Wheelchair Rental
46	旅游大巴	Tour Bus
47	绿道	Greenway
48	免费饮水	Free Drinking Water
49	攀岩	Rock Climbing

续表

序号	中文	英文
50	票价	Ticket Rates〔Ticket 可省略〕或 Fares
51	热门景区	Popular Scenic Spot
52	散客通道	Individual Visitors Passage〔Passage 可省略〕
53	上楼楼梯	Stairway Up〔Stairway 可省略〕
54	生态小道	Eco-Trail
55	手杖租借	Walking Stick Rental
56	狩猎区	Hunting Area
57	水果采摘区	Fruit-Picking Area
58	水上漂流	Drifting
59	水上运动	Aquatic Sports 或 Water Sports
60	投喂区	Feeding Area
61	团队通道	Group Passage〔Passage 可省略〕
62	团体入口；团体检票口	Group Entrance
63	退押金处	Deposit Refund
64	网红打卡地	Popular Photo Spot
65	温泉浴	Hot Spring Bathing

续表

序号	中文	英文
66	下楼楼梯	Stairway Down〔Stairway 可省略〕
67	休闲广场	Leisure Plaza
68	休闲区	Leisure Area
69	学生票：____ 元	Student: ____ Yuan
70	婴儿车租借	Stroller Rental
71	乡村旅游	Rural Tourism
72	行人道	Walkway
73	游客停车场	Visitor Parking 或 Visitors〔用于 Parking 可省略的场合〕
74	游泳池	Swimming Pool
75	雨伞租借	Umbrella Rental
76	照相服务	Photo Services
77	住宿区	Lodging Area
78	租船处	Boat Rental

4. 文化旅游纪念品

序号	中文	英文
1	编织品	Weaving Products 或 Knitted Products
2	玻璃器皿	Glassware
3	瓷器	Porcelain Wares
4	灯饰品	Lighting Decorations
5	雕塑工艺品	Sculpture Crafts
6	发饰	Hair Decorations
7	糕点	Pastries
8	工艺品	Handicraft
9	挂饰	Hanging Decorations
10	家具	Furniture
11	家庭装饰工艺品	Home Decorations
12	甲骨文摆件	Oracle Bone Inscription Ornaments
13	节日装饰品	Holiday Decorations
14	金陵金箔	Jinling Gold Foil
15	金陵折扇	Jinling Folding Fan

续表

序号	中文	英文
16	金饰	Gold Accessories 或 Gold Ornaments（指室内装潢）
17	景泰蓝	Cloisonné Enamel
18	民间工艺品	Folk Crafts
19	木刻	Wood Carvings
20	木制品	Wooden Products
21	南京绒花	Nanjing Ronghua (Velvet Flowers)
22	南京云锦	Nanjing Yunjin Brocade
23	泥塑工艺品	Clay Carving Crafts
24	时尚饰品	Fashion Decorations
25	手工艺品	Artifacts 或 Handicrafts
26	首饰盒	Jewelry Boxes
27	树脂工艺品	Resin Crafts
28	水晶工艺品	Crystal Crafts
29	苏绣	Suzhou Embroidery
30	塑料制品	Plastic Articles
31	炭雕工艺品	Charcoal Carving Crafts

续表

序号	中文	英文
32	唐三彩	Tricolor-Glazed Pottery
33	陶瓷工艺品	Porcelain Crafts
34	天然工艺品	Natural Crafts
35	文房四宝（笔、墨、纸、砚）	Four Treasures of the Study (Brush, Inkstick, Paper and Inkstone)
36	皮件	Leather Products
37	银饰	Silver Ornaments
38	雨花石	Yuhua Pebbles 或 Rain Flower Pebbles
39	珍珠工艺品	Pearl Crafts
40	纸制工艺品	Paper Crafts
41	中国结	Chinese Knots
42	竹制工艺品	Bamboo Crafts
43	装饰品	Decorations
44	装饰纸品	Decorative Paper Grafts
45	字画卷轴	Scrolls of Calligraphy and Paintings

5. 其他文化相关信息

（1）节假日名称

序号	中文	英文
1	除夕	Chinese New Year's Eve
2	春节	The Spring Festival 或 Chinese New Year
3	登山节	Mountain-Climbing Festival
4	端午节	The Dragon-Boat Festival
5	父亲节	Father's Day
6	复活节	Easter
7	感恩节	Thanksgiving Day
8	古尔邦节	Corban Festival
9	国际儿童节（六一儿童节）	International Children's Day (Children's Day)
10	国际劳动妇女节	International Working Women's Day
11	国庆节	National Day
12	护士节	Nurses' Day
13	记者节	Journalists' Day
14	中国人民解放军建军节	The Army Day of the Chinese People's Liberation Army 或 PLA Day

续表

序号	中文	英文
15	教师节	Teachers' Day
16	开斋节	Eid al-Fitr
17	狂欢节	Carnival
18	庙会	Temple Fair
19	母亲节	Mother's Day
20	乞巧节；七夕（中国情人节）	The Qixi Festival (Chinese Valentine's Day)
21	清明节	Tomb-Sweeping Day 或 Qingming Festival
22	情人节	Valentine's Day
23	圣诞节	Christmas Day
24	万圣夜	Halloween
25	国际劳动节（五一节）	International Workers' Day 或 May Day
26	愚人节	April Fools' Day
27	元旦	New Year's Day
28	元宵节	The Lantern Festival
29	植树节	Tree Planting Day
30	中国共产党生日（党的生日）	Anniversary of the Founding of the Communist Party of China (Party's Birthday)

续表

序号	中文	英文
31	中国青年节（五四青年节）	Chinese Youth Day (May Fourth Youth Day)
32	中秋节	The Mid-Autumn Festival 或 The Moon Festival
33	重阳节	The Chongyang Festival 或 The Double Ninth Festival

（2）传统文化领域

序号	中文	英文
1	白局	Nanjing Baiju
2	爆竹	Firecrackers
3	编钟	Chime Bell
4	春联	Spring Festival Couplets
5	道士	Daoist Priest
6	灯会	Lantern Show
7	灯笼	Lantern
8	佛经	Buddhist Scripture
9	佛祖	Buddha

续表

序号	中文	英文
10	功夫	Kungfu
11	和尚	Monk
12	火药	Gunpowder
13	剪纸	Paper Cutting
14	剑术	Chinese Swordsmanship
15	京剧	Peking Opera
16	昆曲	Kunqu Opera
17	尼姑	Nun
18	农历	Lunar Calendar
19	皮影戏	Shadow Puppetry
20	评弹	Pingtan Storytelling
21	菩萨	Bodhisattva
22	气功	Qigong
23	书法	Calligraphy
24	双簧	Two-Man Comic
25	太极拳	Taijiquan

续表

序号	中文	英文
26	五行（金、木、水、火、土）	Five Elements (Metal, Wood, Water, Fire and Earth)
27	舞龙	Dragon Dance
28	舞狮	Lion Dance
29	戏剧脸谱	Theatrical Masks
30	戏曲	Traditional Opera
31	相声	Crosstalk
32	压岁钱	Lucky Money
33	阳历	Solar Calendar
34	印刷术	Movable Type Printing
35	越剧	Yueju Opera
36	杂耍	Variety Show
37	造纸术	Paper Making
38	指南针	Compass
39	笛子（乐器）	Dizi (Chinese Bamboo Flute)
40	二胡（乐器）	Erhu (Chinese Two-Stringed Bowed Instrument)
41	古琴（乐器）	Guqin (Chinese Zither With Seven Strings)

续表

序号	中文	英文
42	古筝（乐器）	Guzheng (Chinese Zither With 21 Strings)
43	鼓（乐器）	Drum
44	管子（乐器）	Guanzi (Chinese Double-Reed End-Blown Bamboo or Wooden Flute)
45	箜篌（乐器）	Konghou (Chinese Harp)
46	琵琶（乐器）	Pipa (Chinese Pear-Shaped Lute Played With Fingers)
47	笙（乐器）	Sheng (Chinese Free Reed Pipe)
48	唢呐（乐器）	Suona (Chinese Double-Reed Horn Noted for Its Loud, High Pitched Sound)
49	箫（乐器）	Xiao (Chinese End-Blown Bamboo Flute)
50	埙（乐器）	Xun (Chinese Egg-Shaped Vessel Flute Made of Clay or Ceramic)
51	扬琴（乐器）	Yangqin (Chinese Dulcimer Played With Bamboo Beaters)
52	中阮（乐器）	Zhongruan (Chinese Tenor-Ranged Lute Played With a Pick or With Fingers)
53	立春（节气）	Beginning of Spring
54	雨水（节气）	Rain Water
55	惊蛰（节气）	Awakening of Insects
56	春分（节气）	Spring Equinox
57	清明（节气）	Pure Brightness

续表

序号	中文	英文
58	谷雨（节气）	Grain Rain
59	立夏（节气）	Beginning of Summer
60	小满（节气）	Grain Buds
61	芒种（节气）	Grain in Ear
62	夏至（节气）	Summer Solstice
63	小暑（节气）	Minor Heat
64	大暑（节气）	Major Heat
65	立秋（节气）	Beginning of Autumn
66	处暑（节气）	End of Heat
67	白露（节气）	White Dew
68	秋分（节气）	Autumn Equinox
69	寒露（节气）	Cold Dew
70	霜降（节气）	Frost’s Descent
71	立冬（节气）	Beginning of Winter
72	小雪（节气）	Minor Snow
73	大雪（节气）	Major Snow

续表

序号	中文	英文
74	冬至（节气）	Winter Solstice
75	小寒（节气）	Minor Cold
76	大寒（节气）	Major Cold

6. 文旅警示指示说明信息

序号	中文	英文
1	保护野生动物	Protect Wildlife
2	打开安全杆	Lift Safety Bar
3	淡季	Low Season 或 Slack Season
4	返回验印	Visitors Re-Entry Sticker Check
5	即将上映	Coming Soon 或 Upcoming Movies
6	禁止乱刻乱画	No Graffiti
7	景区内禁止狩猎	No Hunting
8	缆车最大载重量：____ 人	Maximum Cabin Capacity: ____ People
9	请爱护洞内景观	Please Show Respect for Sights Inside the Cave

续表

序号	中文	英文
10	请爱护古树	Please Show Respect for the Heritage Tree〔tree 应根据实际情况选单数或复数〕
11	请爱护景区设施	Please Show Respect for Public Facilities
12	请爱护文物；保护文物	Please Show Respect for Cultural Relics
13	请将手机调至静音或震动状态	Please Mute Your Mobile Phone
14	请勿触摸	Please Do Not Touch
15	请勿惊吓、戏弄动物	Do Not Disturb Animals
16	请勿录音	No Audio Recording
17	请勿摄像	No Video Recording
18	请勿喂食；请勿投食	No Feeding
19	请在台阶下等候	Please Stand Clear of the Steps
20	请准时入场，对号入座，迟到的观众请待幕间安静时，入场就近入座。	Please arrive on time and take your assigned seat. If you are late, wait for intermission and take the nearest seat.
21	旺季	High Season 或 Peak Season
22	维护生态环境，保护生物多样性	Preserve Ecosystem and Biodiversity
23	未成年人禁止入内	Children Not Allowed
24	谢绝退换	No Refund or Exchange

续表

序号	中文	英文
25	欣赏交响乐曲时，乐曲的乐章之间，请不要鼓掌	Please Do Not Applaud Between Movements
26	演出进行中，请勿大声喧哗或随意走动	Performance in Progress. Please Remain Seated and Keep Quiet
27	展品不外售	Not for Sale
28	珍爱森林，防火为先	Protect Our Forest From Fire

五、教育体育

Part 5 Education and sports

1. 范围

本部分规定了南京市教育体育服务领域英文译写的相关术语和定义、译写要求和方法等。

本部分适用于南京市学校及其他教育机构名称、体育场所名称以及教育体育领域公共服务信息的英文译写。

2. 规范性引用文件

应用本部分内容需参考如下文件。如文件注明日期，则仅注日期的版本适用于本文件。如文件未注日期，则其最新版本（包括所有的修改单）适用于本部分。

汉语拼音方案（1958 年中华人民共和国第一届全国人民代表大会第五次会议审议通过）

GB 17733 地名 标志

GB/T 10001（所有部分）标志用公共信息图形符号

GB/T 16159 汉语拼音正词法基本规则

GB/T 30240.1—2013 公共服务领域英文译写规范（第 1 部分：通则）

GB/T 30240.5—2017 公共服务领域英文译写规范（第 5 部分：体育）

GB/T 30240.6—2017 公共服务领域英文译写规范（第 6 部分：教育）

DB32/T 1446.4—2009 公共场所英文译写规范（第 4 部分：文化体育）

3. 术语和定义

下列术语和定义适用于本部分。

3.1 教育领域公共场所 public educational institutions and facilities

开展教育、教学活动的各级各类学校及校外教育机构和场所。

3.2 体育场所 sports venues and facilities

开展体育竞赛、运动训练、体育教学、全民健身等活动的各类运动场馆。

4. 译写要求

4.1 教育体育领域公共场所中文标识在 GB/T 10001.1 中已经规定了相应的图形符号时，应首先按照标准的规定使用公共信息图形符号。使用国际通用标识符号或图标的，可不提供英文译写。

4.2 教育体育领域公共场所中文标识采用英文译写时，英文单词的大小写应符合本指南第 1 部分的规定；采用汉语拼音标注时，拼写应符合 GB/T 16159 的规定。

5. 译写方法

5.1 教育领域公共场所

5.1.1 综合性大学译作 University，如："南京大学" Nanjing University。大学的二级学院一般译作 School 或 College，如："信息与通信工程学院" College of Information and Communication Engineering。大学设立学部、学院和系三级教学行政管理机构的，学部译作 Faculty，如："信息学部" Faculty of Information Technology。研究生院译作 Graduate School。系译作 Department，

如：“管理科学与工程系”Department of Management Science and Engineering。专科性学院译作 College 或 Institute，艺术类院校及研究性教育机构译作 Academy，职业技术学院译作 Vocational and Technical College。实际使用中按照“名从主人”的原则。

5.1.2　党校译作 Party School，社会主义学院译作 Institute of Socialism，行政学院一般译作 Academy of Governance。

5.1.3　基础教育的学校译作 School。小学译作 Primary School，中学译作 Middle School，初中译作 Junior Middle School，高中译作 Senior Middle School 或 High School，职业高级中学、中等专业学校 Vocational School；高等职业学校 Vocational College。特殊教育类学校译作 Special Education School，老年大学译作 Lifelong Education University。

5.1.4　附属学校需要译出隶属关系时，“附属”译作 Affiliated。如：“南京师范大学附属中学”High School Affiliated to Nanjing Normal University。

5.1.5　作为校外教育机构的青少年活动中心、基地等均译作 Youth Activity Center。少年宫、青年宫的“宫”可以沿用 Palace。

5.1.6　成人教育体系中的业余大学、继续教育学院等译作 College of Continuing Education。社区学校译作 Community School。

5.1.7　通名的修饰或限定成分需译成两个及以上英文单词时，一般置于通名之后，用介词 of 连接，如：“南京邮电大学”Nanjing University of Posts and Telecommunications。修饰或限定成分只有一个英文单词时，可以置于通名之前，如：“南京农业大学”Nanjing Agricultural University。

5.2 学校服务信息

5.2.1 校门应区分不同的情况采用不同的译法。以数字命名的校门用“Gate+阿拉伯数字”的方式译写，如：“一号门”Gate 1。以方位词命名的校门用“方位词+Gate”的方式译写，如：“东门”East Gate。

5.2.2 其他学校服务信息的译写应符合GB/T 30240.1—2013中第5.2条的各项要求。

5.3 体育场所

5.3.1 体育场应区分不同的情况采用不同的译法。包括观众席在内的整个体育场译作Stadium；面积较大，可用于足球、橄榄球、曲棍球、田径等项目比赛和训练的场地译作Field；面积较小，仅用于篮球、网球等项目比赛和训练的场地译作Court。

5.3.2 体育馆译作Indoor Stadium或Gymnasium，如：“南京五台山体育馆”Nanjing Wutaishan Gymnasium。

5.3.3 体育中心应区分不同的规模采用不同的译法。大型体育中心译作Sports Complex；中小型体育中心译作Sports Center；社区体育活动场所可译作Community Sports Center或Community Sports Ground。

5.3.4 水上运动场馆应区分不同的情况采用不同的译法。可用于游泳、跳水、水球等项目比赛和训练的大型室内游泳场馆译作Natatorium；一般的游泳池译作Swimming Pool或Indoor Swimming Pool。

5.3.5 冰雪运动场所应区分不同的情况采用不同的译法。滑冰场所译作Skating Center或Skating Oval或Skating Rink，速滑馆译作Speed Skating Oval，滑雪场译作Ski Resort。

5.3.6 其他体育场馆名称的译写应符合GB/T 30240.1—2013中第5.1条的各项要求。

5.4 体育服务信息

5.4.1 体育场馆的入场门应区分不同的情况采用不同的译法。以数字命名的入场门用“Gate+阿拉伯数字”的方式译写，如：“一号门”Gate 1。以方位词命名的入场门用“方位词+Gate”的方式译写，如：“东门”East Gate。

5.4.2 体育场馆的座位分区应区分不同的情况采用不同的译法。以数字命名的分区用“Zone+阿拉伯数字”或“Section+阿拉伯数字”的方式译写，如：“一区”Zone 1 或 Section 1。以方位词命名的分区用“方位词+Section”的方式译写，如：“东区”East Section。

5.5 体育运动项目和比赛名称

5.5.1 体育运动项目名称的译写应符合国际体育组织的相关规定。

5.5.2 体育比赛名称应区分不同的情况采用不同的译写方法。包含多个项目比赛的综合性运动会译作 Games, Sports Games 或 Sports Meet；单项运动比赛、邀请赛和锦标赛等译作 Tournament 或 Championship。

5.6 其他教育体育服务信息的英文译写应符合 GB/T 30240.1—2013、GB/T 30240.5—2017 和 GB/T 30240.6—2017 的规定。采用英文直接翻译时，应符合国际通用惯例。

教育体育英文译法示例

注：1. 以下词条在各自二级目录下按照汉语拼音字母的顺序排列（若词条以阿拉伯数字或英文字母开头，则置于表首。数字先排，从小到大；字母后排，按照字母表顺序）。

2.“〔 〕”中的内容是对英文译法的解释说明。“（ ）”及其所包含的内容如果是词条的组成部分应保留，如果是词条的缩写、简称或其它同义词语则可根据实际情况选择使用。

3.“/”表示“和”或者“或”，如果是词条的组成部分应保留，如果表示选择关系则根据情况选择使用。“//”表示换行。

1. 教育领域公共场所及服务信息

序号	中文	英文
1	办证处（指借书证）	Card Service
2	报到	Registration
3	报刊阅览室	Newspapers and Periodicals
4	必修课	Compulsory 或 Required Course
5	毕业典礼	Commencement 或 Graduation Ceremony
6	毕业证书	Diploma
7	博士学位证书	Doctoral Degree Certificate

续表

序号	中文	英文
8	操场	Sports Ground〔中小学、大学〕或 Playground〔幼儿园〕
9	成绩报告	Report Booklet
10	成绩单	Transcript
11	成人教育	Adult Education
12	初中	Junior Middle School
13	大礼堂	Auditorium 或 Assembly Hall
14	档案馆	Archives
15	党校	Party School
16	电子工程实验室	Electronics Engineering Laboratory 或 Electronics Engineering Lab
17	电子阅览室	Digital Reading Room
18	多功能教室	Multifunction Classroom
19	多媒体教室	Multimedia Room
20	儿童图书馆	Childrens Library
21	儿童阅览室	Childrens Reading Room
22	辅修	Minor
23	高等职业学校	Vocational College

续表

序号	中文	英文
24	高中	Senior Middle School 或 High School
25	公告栏	Notice Board 或 Bulletin Board
26	公共检索	Catalog Search
27	行政学院	Academy of Governance
28	化学实验室	Chemistry Laboratory 或 Chemistry Lab
29	活动室	Activity Room
30	基础教育	Basic Education
31	基础课	Foundation Courses
32	计算机教室	Computer Room
33	奖学金	Scholarship
34	教师食堂	Faculty Canteen 或 Teachers Canteen
35	教师休息室	Faculty Lounge 或 Teachers Lounge
36	教师宿舍	Faculty Dormitory 或 Teachers Dormitory
37	教学楼	Teaching Building
38	阶梯教室	Terrace Classroom 或 Lecture Theater
39	借书处	Circulation

续表

序号	中文	英文
40	技术学校	Technical School 或 Technical College
41	开学典礼	Opening Ceremony
42	科学技术馆	Science and Technology Museum
43	科学中心	Science Center
44	课程表	Class Schedule 或 Timetable
45	课程设置	Curriculum
46	课外活动	Extracurricular Activities
47	篮球场	Basketball Court
48	留学生公寓	International Student Dormitory
49	美术教室	Art Room
50	旁听生	Visiting Student
51	跑道	Track
52	培养方案	Education Program
53	期刊阅览室	Periodicals Reading Room
54	期末考试	Final Examination
55	期中考试	Mid-Term Examination

续表

序号	中文	英文
56	浅水区	Shallow End
57	青少年活动中心	Youth Activity Center
58	还书处	Book Return
59	少年宫	Childrens Palace
60	少年之家	Childrens Home
61	社会实践	Social Practice
62	社会调查	Social Investigation
63	社区教育	Community Education
64	社区学校	Community School
65	深水区	Deep End
66	生物实验室	Biology Laboratory 或 Biology Lab
67	实验楼	Laboratory Building
68	实验室	Laboratory 或 Lab
69	食堂	Canteen
70	视听教室	Audio-Visual Room
71	视障阅览室	Low Vision Readers Only

续表

序号	中文	英文
72	书法教室	Calligraphy Room
73	数字科技馆	Digital Science and Technology Museum
74	数字图书馆	Digital Library
75	硕士学位证书	Master's Degree Certificate
76	太空馆	Space Hall
77	特殊教育	Special Education
78	特殊教育学校	Special Education School
79	体验馆	Experience Hall
80	体验中心	Experience Center
81	体育器材室	Sports Equipment Room
82	田径场	Track-and-Field Ground
83	听课证	Auditing Permit
84	图书馆	Library
85	图书预定	Book Reservation
86	文献检索服务	Document Retrieval Service
87	舞蹈室	Dancing Room

续表

序号	中文	英文
88	物理实验室	Physics Laboratory 或 Physics Lab
89	小学	Primary School
90	小学教育	Primary〔或 Elementary〕Education
91	中学教育	Secondary Education
92	高等教育	Higher Education
93	校车	School Bus
94	校车车站；班车点	Bus Stop 或 School Bus Stop
95	校车路线图	Bus Route 或 School Bus Route
96	校车运营时间表	Bus Timetable 或 School Bus Timetable
97	校规	School Rules
98	校纪	School Discipline
99	校区平面图	Campus Map
100	校史馆；校史陈列室	____ History Museum〔根据不同的学校性质填入 University、College 或 School〕
101	校训	School Motto
102	校园卡	Campus Card
103	校园卡管理中心	Campus Card Center

续表

序号	中文	英文
104	校园卡自助服务中心	Campus Card Self-Service Center
105	心理咨询室	Psychological Counseling Room
106	新生训练	Orientation Program
107	信息技术实验室	Information Technology Laboratory 或 Information Technology Lab
108	休息室	Lounge
109	宿舍楼	Dormitory
110	选修课	Optional Course 或 Elective Course
111	学费	Tuition
112	学分制	Credit System
113	学期	Semester 或 Term
114	学生会	Student Union
115	学生社团	Clubs
116	学生宿舍	Student Dormitory
117	学生证	Student ID Card
118	学士学位证书	Bachelor's Degree Certificate
119	学术报告厅	Lecture Hall

续表

序号	中文	英文
120	学术讲座	Lecture
121	学位证书	Degree Certificate
122	学习园地	Study Corner
123	研讨会	Seminar
124	业余大学、继续教育学院	College of Continuing Education
125	义务劳动	Voluntary Service
126	音乐室	Music Room
127	游泳馆	Natatorium 或 Swimming Pool
128	预约取书	Reserved Books Pickup
129	阅览部；阅览处；阅览室	Reading Room
130	杂费	Miscellaneous Expenses
131	职业高级中学；中等专业学校	Vocational School
132	职业教育	Vocational Education
133	中学	Middle School
134	主楼	Main Building
135	主修	Major

续表

序号	中文	英文
136	助学金	Student Grant
137	专业课	Specialized Course
138	自习室	Individual Study Room
139	（自助）还书处	Book Drop
140	综合阅览室	General Reading Room
141	足球场	Football Field

2. 高校内设机构名称

序号	中文	英文
1	保卫处	Security Department
2	财务处	Finance Office
3	党支部	CPC Branch
4	国际合作交流处	International Cooperation and Exchange Office
5	后勤处	Logistics Department
6	教务处	Academic Affairs Office

续表

序号	中文	英文
7	科研处	Academic Research Office
8	人事处	Human Resources Office
9	社会主义学院	Institute of Socialism
10	系（大学内）	Department
11	校长办公室	President's Office
12	信息技术学部	Faculty of Information Technology
13	信息与通信工程学院	College of Information and Communication Engineering
14	学生处	Student Affairs Office
15	学院（大学内）	College 或 School
16	研究生院	Graduate School
17	招生办公室	Admissions Office
18	总务处	General Affairs Office

3. 中小学及幼儿园内设机构名称

序号	中文	英文
1	班级	Class

续表

序号	中文	英文
2	初中部	Junior Middle Division
3	高中部	Senior Middle Department
4	教导处	Teaching Affairs Office
5	年级	Grade
6	数学组	Mathematics Teaching Faculty
7	体育组	Physical Education Faculty 或 PE Faculty
8	外语组	Foreign Languages Teaching Faculty
9	小学部	Primary School Division
10	校长室	Principal's Office〔中学〕或 Headmaster's Office〔小学〕
11	艺术组	Art Teaching Faculty
12	英语组	English Teaching Faculty
13	幼儿园大班	Upper Grade (of Kindergarten)
14	幼儿园小班	Lower Grade (of Kindergarten)
15	幼儿园中班	Middle Grade (of Kindergarten)
16	语文组	Chinese Teaching Faculty
17	中学部	Secondary School Division

4. 教育系统人员名称

序号	中文	英文
1	班主任	Class Advisor
2	保育员	Child Carer
3	本科生	Undergraduate Student〔Student 可以省略〕
4	博士生	PhD Student
5	博士生导师	PhD Supervisor
6	大学校长	President
7	导师	Supervisor 或 Adviser 或 Mentor
8	德育主任	Director of Moral Education Office
9	教务主任	Director of Academic Affairs
10	实验员	Laboratory Technician
11	特级教师	Special-Grade Senior Teacher
12	____ 系主任	Chair of ____ Department
13	小学校长	Headmaster〔无论男女〕
14	校友（男 / 女）	Alumnus〔男单〕/ Alumna〔女单〕/ Alumni〔复〕
15	学院院长	Dean of College 或 Dean of School

续表

序号	中文	英文
16	研究生	Graduate Student 或 Postgraduate
17	研究生导师	Supervisor
18	院士	Academician
19	中学校长	Principal

5. 驻宁高校名称

序号	中文	英文
1	东南大学	Southeast University
2	河海大学	Hohai University
3	江苏第二师范学院	Jiangsu Second Normal University
4	江苏警官学院	Jiangsu Police Institute
5	金陵科技学院	Jinling Institute of Technology
6	南京财经大学	Nanjing University of Finance & Economics
7	南京城市职业学院	Nanjing City Vocational College
8	南京大学	Nanjing University

续表

序号	中文	英文
9	南京工程学院	Nanjing Institute of Technology
10	南京工业大学	Nanjing Tech University
11	南京工业职业技术大学	Nanjing Vocational University of Industry Technology
12	南京航空航天大学	Nanjing University of Aeronautics and Astronautics
13	南京机电职业技术学院	Nanjing Vocational Institute of Mechatronic Technology
14	南京警察学院	Nanjing Police University
15	南京理工大学	Nanjing University of Science & Technology
16	南京林业大学	Nanjing Forestry University
17	南京农业大学	Nanjing Agricultural University
18	南京审计大学	Nanjing Audit University
19	南京师范大学	Nanjing Normal University
20	南京特殊教育师范学院	Nanjing Normal University of Special Education
21	南京体育学院	Nanjing Sport Institute
22	南京晓庄学院	Nanjing Xiaozhuang University
23	南京信息工程大学	Nanjing University of Information Science & Technology
24	南京医科大学	Nanjing Medical University

续表

序号	中文	英文
25	南京艺术学院	Nanjing University of the Arts
26	南京邮电大学	Nanjing University of Posts and Telecommunications
27	南京中医药大学	Nanjing University of Chinese Medicine
28	中国药科大学	China Pharmaceutical University

6. 南京市属学校名称

序号	中文	英文
1	南京财经高等职业技术学校	Nanjing Vocational College of Finance and Economics
2	南京高等职业技术学校	Nanjing Technical Vocational College
3	南京师范大学附属中学	High School Affiliated to Nanjing Normal University
4	南京师范大学附属中学实验初级中学	Experimental Junior Section, High School Affiliated to Nanjing Normal University
5	南京市第一中学	Nanjing No.1 Middle School
6	南京市建宁中学	Nanjing Jianning Middle School
7	南京市金陵中学	Nanjing Jinling High School
8	南京市聋人学校	Nanjing School for the Deaf

续表

序号	中文	英文
9	南京市盲人学校	Nanjing School for the Blind
10	南京市中华中学	Nanjing Zhonghua High School
11	南京外国语学校	Nanjing Foreign Language School
12	南京卫生高等职业技术学校	Nanjing Vocational Health College

7. 体育场馆名称

序号	中文	英文
1	棒球场	Baseball Field
2	保龄球馆	Bowling Alley
3	大型体育中心	Sports Complex
4	地掷球场	Bocce Court
5	高尔夫球场	Golf Course
6	旱冰场；轮滑场	Roller Skating Rink
7	滑冰场	Skating Center 或 Skating Rink
8	滑雪场	Ski Resort

续表

序号	中文	英文
9	击剑馆	Fencing Hall
10	举重馆	Weightlifting Gym
11	卡丁车场	Karting Track
12	篮球馆	Basketball Gym
13	垒球场	Softball Field
14	门球场	Gateball Court 或 Croquet Court
15	排球场	Volleyball Court
16	排球馆	Volleyball Gym
17	攀岩场	Climbing Gym 或 Rock Climbing Ground
18	乒乓球馆	Table Tennis Gym
19	棋牌俱乐部	Board Games Club
20	曲棍球场	Hockey Field
21	全民健身活动中心	Community Fitness Center
22	拳击馆	Boxing Gym
23	柔道馆	Judo Gym
24	山地自行车赛场	Mountain Bike Racing Track

续表

序号	中文	英文
25	社区体育活动场所	Community Sports Center 或 Community Sports Ground
26	射击馆	Shooting Range
27	射箭场	Archery Range
28	手球场	Handball Court
29	手球馆	Handball Gym
30	摔跤馆	Wrestling Gym
31	速滑馆	Speed Skating Oval
32	台球馆	Billiard Hall
33	跆拳道馆	Taekwondo Gym
34	体育公园	Sports Park
35	体育馆	Gymnasium 或 Gym
36	网球场	Tennis Court
37	武术馆	Wushu Gym 或 Martial Arts Gym
38	瑜伽馆	Yoga Gym
39	羽毛球馆	Badminton Gym
40	中小型体育中心	Sports Center

8. 体育运动项目名称

序号	中文	英文
1	拔河	Tug of War
2	棒球	Baseball
3	保龄球	Bowling
4	壁球	Squash
5	电子竞技	Electronic Sports 或 E-Sports
6	钓鱼	Angling
7	浮潜	Snorkeling
8	高尔夫球	Golf
9	滑水	Water Skiing 或 Water Ski
10	滑翔	Gliding
11	击剑	Fencing
12	健美操	Aerobics
13	毽球	Shuttlecock
14	街舞	Street Dance
15	竞技体操	Artistic Gymnastics

续表

序号	中文	英文
16	举重	Weightlifting
17	卡巴迪	Kabaddi
18	空手道	Karate
19	篮球	Basketball
20	垒球	Softball
21	龙舟	Dragon Boat
22	马术	Equestrian
23	门球	Gateball 或 Croquet
24	摩托艇	Motorboat
25	排球	Volleyball
26	皮划艇	Canoe
27	乒乓球	Table Tennis
28	桥牌	Bridge
29	曲棍球	Hockey
30	拳击	Boxing
31	柔道	Judo

续表

序号	中文	英文
32	柔术	Jujitsu
33	赛艇	Rowing
34	射击	Shooting
35	射箭	Archery
36	深潜；水肺潜水	Scuba Diving
37	手球	Handball
38	摔跤	Wrestling
39	双排轮滑	Roller Skating
40	水球	Water Polo
41	台球	Billiards
42	跆拳道	Taekwondo
43	藤球	Sepaktakraw
44	体操	Gymnastics
45	田径	Athletics
46	跳伞	Parachuting
47	跳水	Diving

续表

序号	中文	英文
48	铁人三项	Triathlon
49	网球	Tennis
50	围棋	Go
51	武道	Martial Arts
52	武术	Wushu
53	现代五项	Modern Pentathlon
54	艺术体操	Rhythmic Gymnastics
55	游泳	Swimming
56	羽毛球	Badminton
57	直排轮滑	Roller Blading
58	掷球	Boules
59	自行车运动	Cycling
60	足球	Football 或 Soccer

9. 体育场馆设施名称

序号	中文	英文
1	安保封闭区	Enclosed Zone
2	安保指挥中心	Security Command Center
3	裁判台	Referee Stand
4	裁判席	Referee Seats 或 Umpire Seats〔后者用于网球、棒球裁判〕
5	裁判员室	Referee Room 或 Umpire Room〔后者用于网球、棒球裁判〕
6	场馆媒体中心	Venue Media Center
7	场馆示意图	Venue Map
8	场馆通信中心	Venue Communication Center
9	场馆注册办公室	Venue Accreditation Office
10	传输控制室	Transmission Control Room
11	单号入口	Odd Number Entrance
12	等候区	Waiting Area
13	电视评论席	TV Commentators
14	电视转播区	TV Broadcast Zone
15	观众入口	Spectator Entrance 或 Spectators〔用于 Entrance 可省略的场合〕

续表

序号	中文	英文
16	观众通道	Spectator Passage
17	贵宾通道	VIP Passage
18	贵宾席	VIP
19	混合采访区	Mixed Zone
20	记者休息室	Media Lounge
21	检录处	Call Area
22	竞赛场地	Field of Play
23	看台；观众席	Spectator Area
24	客队休息室	Guest Team Lounge 或 Visitor Team Lounge
25	露天看台	Bleachers
26	媒体工作间	Media Workroom
27	媒体席	Press Zone
28	人员验证点	Accreditation Check Point
29	散场通道	EXIT 或 Exit
30	摄影记者区	Photo Zone
31	双号入口	Even Number Entrance

续表

序号	中文	英文
32	替补席	Substitutes Bench
33	通道；过道（座位区之间）	Aisle
34	通行区；场馆公众区	Front of House (FOH)
35	团体入口	Group Entrance
36	无障碍座位	Accessible Seats 或 Barrier Free Seats
37	新闻发布厅	Press Conference Hall
38	新闻媒体区	Media Area
39	新闻运行区	Press Operation Zone
40	兴奋剂检测中心	Anti-Doping Laboratory
41	兴奋剂检查室	Doping Control Station
42	运动员席	Athletes' Seats
43	运动员休息室	Athletes Lounge
44	运动员医疗站	Athlete Medical Station
45	运动员专用通道	Athletes Passage 或 Athletes Only〔用于 Passage 可省略的场合〕
46	运营区 / 场馆工作区	Back of House (BOH)
47	主队休息室	Host Team Lounge 或 Home Team Lounge

续表

序号	中文	英文
48	主体育场	Main Stadium
49	主席台（体育场）	VIP Stand
50	主新闻中心	Main Press Center

10. 南京市体育场馆名称

序号	中文	英文
1	东南大学九龙湖体育馆	Southeast University Jiulonghu Gymnasium
2	江苏省五台山体育中心	Jiangsu Wutaishan Sports Center
3	南京奥林匹克体育中心	Nanjing Olympic Sports Center
4	南京大学方肇周体育馆	Nanjing University Fang Zhaozhou Gymnasium
5	南京青奥体育公园	Nanjing Youth Olympic Games Sports Park
6	南京师范大学游泳馆	Nanjing Normal University Natatorium
7	南京中央体育场	Nanjing Central Stadium

六、医疗卫生

Part 6 Health and medicine

1. 范围

本部分规定了南京市医疗卫生领域英文译写的相关术语和定义、译写要求和方法等。

本部分适用于南京市医疗卫生机构名称、医疗服务信息、医院科室名称的英文译写。

2. 规范性引用文件

应用本部分内容需参考如下文件。如文件注明日期，则仅注日期的版本适用于本文件。如文件未注日期，则其最新版本（包括所有的修改单）适用于本部分。

汉语拼音方案（1958 年中华人民共和国第一届全国人民代表大会第五次会议审议通过）

GB/T 10001（所有部分）标志用公共信息图形符号

GB/T 30240.1—2013 公共服务领域英文译写规范（第 1 部分：通则）

GB/T 30240.7—2017 公共服务领域英文译写规范（第 7 部分：医疗卫生）

DB32/T 1446.5—2009 公共场所英文译写规范（第 5 部分：医疗卫生）

3. 术语和定义

下列术语和定义适用于本部分。

3.1 医疗卫生机构 health care and medical institution

具有医疗、预防、保健、医学教育和科研功能的单位或机构。

3.2 医疗服务信息 medical service information

向公众提供医疗、保健、预防等功能的各类功能性提示信息。

3.3 医院科室名称 hospital department

医院内按照专业领域划分的提供专业医疗服务和治疗方案的部门。

4. 译写要求

4.1 医疗卫生领域公共场所中文标识在 GB/T 10001.1 中已经规定了相应的图形符号时，应首先按照标准的规定使用公共信息图形符号。使用国际通用标识符号或图标的，可不提供英文译写。

4.2 医疗卫生领域公共场所中文标识采用英文译写时，英文单词的大小写应符合本指南第 1 部分的规定；采用汉语拼音标注时，拼写应符合 GB/T 16159 的规定。

5. 译写方法

5.1 医疗卫生机构

5.1.1 医院译作 Hospital，诊所、卫生室、医务室等译作 Clinic，研究所译作 Institute，实验室译作 Laboratory 或 Lab，疗养院译作 Sanatorium 或 Convalescent Home，康复医院译作 Rehabilitation Hospital，急救中心译作 Emergency Medical Center，疾病预防控

制中心译作 Center for Disease Control and Prevention (CDC)；社区卫生服务中心译作 Community Healthcare Center，血液中心译作 Blood Center，卫生监督所译作 Health Inspection Center，护理医院一般译作 Nursing Home。

5.1.2　中心医院译作 Central Hospital，人民医院译作 People's Hospital；妇产科医院译作 Women's Hospital，儿童医院译作 Children's Hospital；口腔医院译作 Stomatology Hospital 或 Oral Hospital；社区卫生服务中心译作 Community Health (Healthcare) Center。

5.1.3　医院的分院需要译出隶属关系时，采用“专名 +Branch，总院名称”的形式，如：“南京市第一医院河西分院”Hexi Branch, Nanjing No.1 Hospital。

5.1.4　大学附属医院需要译出隶属关系时，“附属”译作 Affiliated，也可省去不译，将大学名称置于医院名称之后，中间用“,”隔开，如：“南京医科大学附属妇产医院”The Maternity Hospital Affiliated to Nanjing Medical University 或 The Maternity Hospital, Nanjing Medical University。

5.1.5　医保定点医疗机构译作 Medical Insurance Designated Hospital 或 Medical Insurance Designated Clinic，医保定点药房译作 Medical Insurance Designated Pharmacy。

5.1.6　中医译作 Traditional Chinese Medicine (TCM)，在指代高校或医院时可译作 Chinese Medicine。

5.1.7　其他医疗卫生机构的译写应符合 GB/T 30240.1—2013 中第 5.1 条的各项要求。

5.2　医疗服务信息

5.2.1　楼、科、室等医院内部功能设施译作 Building、Department 和 Room，可根据设置区域的远近选择翻译或省略翻译。设置在综合性指示标识中（如挂号大厅或候诊区），用于指示远端所处方位时应当译出。如：门诊楼译作 Outpatient Building，儿科译作 Pediatrics Department，作业疗法室译作 Occupational Therapy Room。设置在楼、科、室的门上或门口，用于指示近端所在处所时可以不翻译。如：门诊楼译作 Outpatients，儿科译作 Pediatrics，作业疗法室译作 Occupational Therapy。但当此类功能性室或房间前面的限定修饰成分为独词，有可能引起歧义时，Building、Department 或 Room 不能省略，如："手术室" Operating Room。

5.2.2　针对特殊疾病或特殊需求而设立的不同类别的门诊译作 Clinic，且不能省略。如：发热门诊译作 Fever Clinic，腹泻门诊译作 Diarrhea Clinic，专家门诊译作 Senior Specialist Clinic。

5.2.3　病房译作 Ward，如："烧伤病房" Burns Ward。

5.2.4　医疗功能设施涉及许多专业词汇时，按国际通用表示方法翻译，如："重症监护室" Intensive Care Unit (ICU)。

5.2.5　医院的咨询台或具有咨询功能的服务台一般译作 Information 或 Reception，急诊科的分诊台译作 Triage。

5.2.6　其他医疗服务信息的译写应符合 GB/T 30240.1—2013 中第 5.2 条的各项要求。

5.2.7　医院科室的译写应遵循医学术语规范。

5.3　其他医疗卫生服务信息的英文译写应符合 GB/T 30240.1—2013 和 GB/T 30240.7—2017 的规定。采用英文直接翻译时，应符合国际通用惯例。

医疗卫生英文译法示例

注：1. 以下词条在各自二级目录下按照汉语拼音字母的顺序排列（若词条以阿拉伯数字或英文字母开头，则置于表首。数字先排，从小到大；字母后排，按照字母表顺序）。

2. “〔 〕”中的内容是对英文译法的解释说明。“（ ）”及其所包含的内容如果是词条的组成部分应保留，如果是词条的缩写、简称或其它同义词语则可根据实际情况选择使用。

3. “／”表示“和”或者“或”，如果是词条的组成部分应保留，如果表示选择关系则根据情况选择使用。“//”表示换行。

1. 医疗卫生机构名称

序号	中文	英文
1	____ 附属医院	Affiliated Hospital to ____ 或 Affiliated Hospital With ____
2	传染病防治院；传染病医院	Infectious Diseases Hospital
3	儿童医院	Children’s Hospital
4	耳鼻喉科医院	Ear, Nose and Throat Hospital (ENT Hospital)
5	放射医学研究所	Radiation Medicine Institute
6	肺科医院	Lung Hospital
7	妇产科医院	Women’s Hospital

续表

序号	中文	英文
8	妇幼保健院	Women's Hospital 或 Maternity Hospital
9	肝胆外科医院	Hepatobiliary Surgery Hospital
10	肛肠医院	Proctology Hospital
11	高血压研究所	Hypertension Research Institute
12	公共卫生临床中心	Public Health Clinical Center
13	公共卫生医疗中心	Public Health Medical Center
14	红十字会	Red Cross Society
15	护理医院	Nursing Home 或 Nursing Hospital
16	急救中心	Emergency Medical Center
17	疾病预防控制中心	Center for Disease Control and Prevention
18	健康教育所	Health Education Center
19	精神卫生医院	Mental Health Hospital 或 Psychiatric Hospital
20	康复医院	Rehabilitation Hospital
21	口腔病防治院	Oral Clinic
22	口腔医院	Stomatology Hospital 或 Oral Hospital
23	疗养院	Sanatorium 或 Convalescent Home

续表

序号	中文	英文
24	临床检验中心	Clinic Laboratory Center
25	免疫学研究所	Immunology Institute
26	脑科医院	Brain Hospital
27	内分泌研究所	Endocrinology Institute
28	皮肤病医院	Dermatology Hospital
29	人民医院	People’s Hospital
30	伤骨科研究所	Orthopaedic Traumatology Institute
31	社区卫生服务中心	Community Healthcare Center
32	社区卫生服务中心医疗服务站	Community Healthcare Clinic
33	社区诊所	Community Clinic
34	生物制品研究所	Research Institute of Biological Products
35	卫生监督所	Health Inspection Center
36	卫生室；医务室	Clinic 或 Medical Room
37	心血管研究所	Cardiovascular Medicine Institute
38	性病医院	STD Hospital
39	胸科医院	Chest Hospital

续表

序号	中文	英文
40	血液管理办公室	Blood Donation Management Office
41	牙病防治院（所）	Dental Clinic
42	研究所	Institute
43	眼病防治院（所）	Eye Clinic
44	眼科医院	Eye Hospital
45	医保办	Medical Insurance Office
46	医保定点药房	Medical Insurance Designated Pharmacy
47	医保定点医疗机构	Medical Insurance Designated Hospital 或 Medical Insurance Designated Clinic
48	医疗急救中心	Medical Emergency Center
49	医院	Hospital
50	针灸经络研究所	Acupuncture and Meridian Research Institute
51	诊所	Clinic
52	职业病防治院	Occupational Health Clinic
53	中心医院	Central Hospital
54	中医卫生监督	TCM Sanitary Inspection
55	中医院	Traditional Chinese Medicine Hospital 或 Chinese Medicine Hospital

续表

序号	中文	英文
56	肿瘤研究所	Oncology Institute
57	肿瘤医院	Oncology Hospital

2. 医院功能设施及名称

序号	中文	英文
1	半污染区	Buffer Area
2	标本登记处	Specimen Registration
3	标本接收处	Specimen Collection
4	病房；病区	Ward
5	病房楼	Inpatient Building
6	产房	Delivery Room
7	冲片室	Film Developing Room
8	抽血处	Blood Sampling
9	出入院办理处	Admission and Discharge
10	出院手续办理处	Discharge

续表

序号	中文	英文
11	处方处	Prescription
12	登记处	Registry
13	第 ____ 诊室	Consulting Room ____
14	儿童重症监护室	Pediatric Intensive Care Unit (Pediatric ICU)
15	放标本处	Specimens
16	非医用垃圾存放处	Non-Medical Waste
17	副院长办公室	Vice President's Office
18	高压氧室；高压氧舱	Hyperbaric Oxygen Chamber
19	隔离区	Isolation Area
20	隔离取血室	Isolated Blood Sampling Room
21	挂号、收费处	Registration and Cashier
22	挂号处	Registration
23	观察室	Observation Room
24	冠心病重症监护室	Coronary Care Unit (CCU)
25	盥洗区	Wash Area
26	候诊观察室	Waiting and Observation Room

续表

序号	中文	英文
27	候诊区	Waiting Area
28	护理部	Nursing Department
29	护士站	Nurse Station
30	划价处；药品划价	Pricing
31	化验室	Laboratory 或 Lab
32	换药室	Dressing Room
33	会客区	Reception Area
34	急诊办公室	Emergency Department Office
35	急诊分诊台	Triage
36	急诊楼	Emergency Building（Building 可省略）
37	急诊室	Emergency Department
38	检查、化验等候区	Lab Test Waiting Area
39	检查室	Examination Room
40	叫号台	Calling Desk
41	接待处；服务台	Reception 或 Information
42	静脉采血处	Venous Blood Sampling

续表

序号	中文	英文
43	救护车	Ambulance
44	就诊区	Outpatient Area
45	麻醉室	Anesthesia Room
46	门诊部	Outpatient Department 或 Outpatients〔用于 Department 可省略的场合〕
47	门诊煎药处	Outpatient Decoction Service
48	门诊楼	Outpatient Building 或 Outpatients〔Building 可省略〕
49	男诊室	Men's Consulting Room
50	女诊室	Women's Consulting Room
51	拍片室；摄片室	Radiography Room
52	配餐室	Meal Preparation Room
53	配液室	Infusion Preparation Room
54	抢救室	Emergency Room 或 Resuscitation Room
55	亲友等候区	Visitors Waiting Area
56	亲友告别室	Bereavement Room
57	清创室	Wound Care Room 或 Debridement Room
58	清洁区	Sterile Area

续表

序号	中文	英文
59	取报告处	Report Collection
60	取检查、化验结果处	Lab Report Collection
61	烧伤病房	Burns Ward
62	收费处	Cashier 或 Payment
63	手术室	Operating Room
64	手术室专用电梯	Operating Room Only〔用于 Elevator 可省略的场合〕
65	输液室	Infusion Room
66	苏醒室；恢复室	Recovery Room
67	胎儿监护室	Fetus Monitoring Room
68	太平间；停尸房	Mortuary 或 Morgue
69	污染区	Contaminated Area
70	污物间	Soiled Articles Disposal Room
71	无偿献血车	Voluntary Blood Donation Vehicle
72	无偿献血屋	Voluntary Blood Donation Station
73	现场抢救区	On-Site Emergency Care
74	献血后休息区	Donors Rest Lounge

续表

序号	中文	英文
75	献血前等候区	Donors Waiting Lounge
76	献血前检测区	Donors Blood Test Area
77	献血咨询登记处	Donation Counseling and Registration
78	消毒产品检验受理处	Sterile Items Test Registration
79	心脏重症监护室	Cardiac Care Unit (CCU)
80	新生儿重症监护室	Neonatal Intensive Care Unit (NICU)
81	宣教室	Health Education Room
82	血库	Blood Bank
83	血液采集区	Blood Collection Area
84	血液中心	Blood Center
85	药房；西药房；中西药房	Pharmacy
86	医保定点药店	Medical Insurance Designated Pharmacy
87	医护办公室	Staff Office
88	医护部	Medical and Nursing Department
89	医技楼	Medical Technology Building〔Building 可省略〕
90	医疗保险管理办公室	Medical Insurance Management Office

续表

序号	中文	英文
91	医疗急救电话 120	First Aid // Call 120
92	医疗纠纷处理办公室	Complaints Office
93	医生办公室	Doctor's Office
94	医用电梯	Medical Use Only〔用于 Elevator 可省略的场合〕
95	医用垃圾存放处	Medical Waste
96	医院行政办公室	Hospital Administration Office
97	乙肝病毒携带者诊室	HBV Carriers Consulting Room
98	营养室	Nutrition Room
99	用药咨询处	Medical Consultation
100	预防保健科	Preventive Medicine Department
101	预检处；先分诊后挂号	Triage Before Registration
102	预约处	Appointments
103	院感科	Hospital-Acquired Infection Control Department
104	院内小卖部	Store
105	院史馆	Hospital Museum
106	院长办公室	President's Office

续表

序号	中文	英文
107	院总值班室	Chief Duty Room
108	诊室	Consulting Room
109	值班室	Duty Room
110	治疗室	Treatment Room
111	中草药房	Herbal Pharmacy
112	中药房	TCM Pharmacy
113	重症监护室	Intensive Care Unit (ICU)
114	住院部	Inpatient Department
115	住院手续办理处；住院登记处	Admission
116	注射室	Injection Room
117	注射输液室	Injection and Infusion Room
118	自助报告打印区	Self-Service Report Printing
119	自助挂号；自助挂号机	Self-Service Registration Machine〔Machine 可省略〕
120	自助预约机	Self-Service Appointment Machine〔Machine 可省略〕
121	作业疗法室	Occupational Therapy Room

3. 医院科室名称

序号	中文	英文
1	病理科	Pathology Department
2	不孕症门诊	Infertility Clinic
3	产科	Obstetrics Department
4	超声科	Ultrasonography Lab〔Lab 可省略〕
5	传染科	Infectious Diseases Department
6	儿科	Pediatrics Department
7	儿科门诊	Pediatrics Clinic
8	儿内科	Pediatric Internal Medicine Department
9	儿外科	Pediatric Surgery Department
10	耳鼻（咽）喉科	Otolaryngology Department 或 Ear, Nose and Throat Department (ENT Department)
11	发热门诊	Fever Clinic
12	放射介入科	Radioactive Intervention Department
13	放射科	Radiology Department
14	肥胖症门诊	Obesity Clinic
15	风湿科	Rheumatology Department

续表

序号	中文	英文
16	风湿免疫科	Rheumatology and Immunology Department
17	妇科	Gynecology Department
18	妇女保健科	Womens Health Care Department
19	腹腔镜外科	Laparoscope Surgery Department
20	腹泻门诊	Diarrhea Clinic
21	肝胆科	Hepatology Department
22	肝胆外科	Hepatological Surgery Department
23	肝炎科	Hepatitis Department
24	肛肠科	Proctology Department
25	高血压科	Hypertension Department
26	隔离门诊	Isolation Clinic
27	更年期门诊	Menopause Clinic
28	骨科；骨伤科	Orthopedics Department
29	核医学科	Nuclear Medicine Department
30	呼吸内科	Respiratory Medicine Department
31	护理门诊	Nursing Clinic

续表

序号	中文	英文
32	检验科	Clinical Lab
33	健康管理中心	Health Management Center
34	介入科	Intervention Department
35	戒毒科	Drug Rehabilitation Department 或 Drug Rehab Department
36	精神科	Psychiatry Department
37	康复科	Rehabilitation Department
38	康复医学科	Rehabilitation Medicine Department
39	口腔颌面医学影像科	Oral and Maxillofacial Radiology
40	口腔科	Stomatology Department
41	口腔科门诊	Stomatology Clinic
42	口腔黏膜病科	Oral Mucosal Disease
43	口腔外科	Stomatology Surgery Department
44	口腔种植科	Oral Implantology
45	老年病科	Geriatrics Department
46	麻醉科	Anesthesiology Department
47	泌尿科	Urology Department

续表

序号	中文	英文
48	免疫科	Immunology Department
49	男科；男性科	Andrology Department
50	内分泌科	Endocrinology Department
51	内科	Internal Medicine Department
52	皮肤病门诊	Dermatology Clinic
53	皮肤科	Dermatology Department
54	普通内科；通用内科	General Internal Medicine Department
55	普通外科	General Surgery Department
56	器官移植科	Organ Transplantation Department
57	伤科	Traumatology Department
58	烧伤科	Burns Department
59	烧伤门诊	Burns Clinic
60	神经内科	Neurology Department
61	神经外科	Neurosurgery Department
62	肾病科	Nephrology Department
63	特需门诊	Special Need Clinic

续表

序号	中文	英文
64	特约门诊	Special Appointment Clinic
65	疼痛科	Pain Mangement Department
66	消化科	Gastroenterology Department
67	心身医学科	Psychosomatic Medicine Departmant
68	牙周病科	Periodontics Department
69	医学检验科	Medical Laboratory Department
70	营养科	Nutrition Department
71	营养门诊	Nutrition Clinic
72	预防医学科；治未病科	Preventive Medicine Department
73	预约门诊	Advance Appointment Clinic
74	镇痛门诊	Pain Clinic
75	职业病科	Occupational Diseases Department
76	职业病咨询门诊	Occupational Health Consulting Clinic
77	职业健康科	Occupational Health Department
78	痔科	Hemorrhoid Department
79	中医骨病治疗科	TCM Orthopedics Department

续表

序号	中文	英文
80	中医理疗科	TCM Physiotherapy Department
81	中医门诊	TCM Clinic
82	中医推拿科	TCM Massage Department
83	肿瘤科	Oncology Department
84	专家门诊	Senior Specialist Clinic
85	专科门诊	Specialist Clinic
86	综合治疗科	Integrated Therapy Department

4. 检查化验项目名称

序号	中文	英文
1	B 超	B-Mode Ultrasound
2	CT 增强扫描	Contrast-Enhanced CT Scan
3	X 光摄片	X-Ray Radiography
4	艾滋病初筛实验	HIV Screening 或 HIV/AIDS Screening
5	白带化验	Leucorrhea Test

续表

序号	中文	英文
6	白带检查	Leucorrhea Examination
7	彩超	Color Ultrasound
8	肠镜检查	Enteroscopy
9	常规化验	Routine Test
10	动态心电图	Dynamic Electrocardiogram (DCG) 或 Holter Monitor
11	动态血压检查	Ambulatory Blood Pressure Monitoring (ABPM)
12	断层扫描（CT）	CT Scan
13	断层扫描（发射单光子计算机）	Emission Computed Tomography (ECT)
14	儿保化验	Child Care Test
15	肺功能检查	Pulmonary Function Test
16	粪便化验	Excrement Test
17	妇科化验	Gynecological Test
18	功能检查	Function Test
19	宫颈冷冻	Cervical Cryotherapy
20	骨密度检测	Bone Mineral Density Test
21	核磁共振	Magnetic Resonance Imaging (MRI)

续表

序号	中文	英文
22	红外线扫描	Infrared Ray
23	口腔放射	Oral Radiology
24	快速检测	Rapid Test
25	量血压	Blood Pressure Measurement
26	免疫检查	Immunoassay
27	脑、肌电图	Electroencephalogram (EEG) and Electromyogram (EMG)
28	内窥镜检查	Endoscopy
29	尿液化验	Urine Test
30	妊高症监测	Gestational Hypertension Monitoring
31	乳腺摄片	Galactophore Radiography
32	数字牙片	Digital Dental Film
33	体温测量	Temperature Taking
34	听力测试	Audiometry
35	透视	Fluoroscopy 或 X-Ray
36	胃肠电图	Electrogastrogram (EGG)
37	胃镜检查	Gastroscopy

续表

序号	中文	英文
38	胃十二指肠镜检查	Gastroduodenoscopy
39	心电图	Electrocardiogram (ECG)
40	心理测验	Psychological Test
41	心脏超声波	Cardiac Ultrasound Scan 或 Echocardiography
42	血气分析	Arterial Blood Gas Analysis
43	牙片	Dental Film
44	眼科验光	Optometry
45	阴超	Transvaginal Ultrasound
46	支气管镜检查	Enteroscopy
47	智力测量	Intelligence Assessment

5. 医疗措施名称

序号	中文	英文
1	艾条灸	Moxa Stick Moxibustion
2	拔罐疗法	Cupping Therapy

续表

序号	中文	英文
3	芳香疗法	Aromatherapy
4	放疗	Radiation Oncology 或 Radiotherapy
5	高压氧治疗	Hyperbaric Oxygen Therapy
6	功能训练	Functional Training
7	骨髓移植	Bone Marrow Transplantation
8	刮痧疗法	Gua Sha 或 Scraping Therapy
9	禁食疗法	Fasting Therapy
10	理疗	Physical Therapy 或 Physiotherapy
11	埋针疗法；皮内针疗法	Needle-Embedding Therapy
12	热敷	Fomentation
13	弱视治疗	Amblyopia Treatment
14	三联疗法	Triple Therapy
15	食疗法	Food Therapy
16	透析	Dialysis
17	推拿	Tuina 或 Manipulation
18	温针灸	Warm-Needling Moxibustion

续表

序号	中文	英文
19	心导管术	Cardiac Catheterization
20	心理治疗	Psychotherapy
21	新生儿水疗抚触	Neonatal Hydrotherapy and Massage
22	序贯疗法	Sequential Therapy
23	悬灸	Suspended Moxibustion
24	穴位敷贴	Acupoint Application Therapy
25	穴位埋线	Catgut-Embedding Therapy
26	穴位注射	Point Injection
27	血透	Hemodialysis
28	意疗法	Imagery Therapy
29	预防接种	Prophylactic Vaccination
30	针灸	Acupuncture
31	针灸疗法	Acupuncture and Moxibustion Therapy
32	中医科按摩	TCM Massage Therapy
33	助听器验配	Hearing Aid Fitting
34	钴 60 治疗；同位素治疗	Cobalt-60 Treatment 或 Isotope Treatment

6. 医学保障设施名称

序号	中文	英文
1	病案室；病史室	Medical Records Room
2	病毒实验室	Virus Analysis Lab
3	操作室	Procedure Room
4	毒理实验室	Toxicology Lab
5	放射防护	Radiation Protection
6	放射免疫实验室	Radioimmunoassay Lab (RIA Lab)
7	分子生物学实毀室	Molecular Biology Lab
8	供应保障区	Storage and Supply Area
9	供应保障组	Supply Team
10	供应室	Storage and Supply Room
11	免疫实验室	Immunoassay Lab
12	生化实验室	Biochemistry Lab
13	实验区	Laboratory Area
14	实验室	Laboratory 或 Lab
15	微量元素实验室	Trace Element Lab

续表

序号	中文	英文
16	微生物实验室	Microbiology Lab
17	细胞化验室	Cell Lab
18	细菌培养室	Bacterial Culture Lab
19	细菌室	Bacteriology Lab
20	血液实验室	Blood Analysis Lab
21	药械科	Drug and Equipment Department
22	疫苗接种室	Vaccination Room

7. 南京市医疗卫生机构名称

序号	中文	英文
1	东南大学附属中大医院	Zhongda Hospital of Southeast University
2	鼓楼医院	Nanjing Drum Tower Hospital (Gulou Hospital)
3	江苏省第二中医院（南京中医药大学第二附属医院）	Jiangsu No.2 Hospital of Chinese Medicine (No. 2 Hospital Affiliated to Nanjing University of Chinese Medicine)
4	江苏省妇幼保健院（江苏省人民医院妇幼分院）	Jiangsu Women and Children's Health Hospital (Women and Children's Health Branch, Jiangsu People's Hospital)
5	江苏省人民医院（南京医科大学第一附属医院）	Jiangsu People's Hospital (No.1 Hospital Affiliated to Nanjing Medical University)

续表

序号	中文	英文
6	江苏省中西医结合医院（中国中医科学院江苏分院，江苏省中医药研究院，南京中医药大学附属中西医结合医院）	Jiangsu Hospital of Integrated Traditional Chinese and Western Medicine (Jiangsu Branch, China Academy of Chinese Medical Sciences / Jiangsu Academy of Traditional Chinese Medicine / The Affiliated Hospital of Integrated Traditional Chinese and Western Medicine of Nanjing University of Chinese Medicine)
7	江苏省中医院（南京中医药大学附属医院）	Jiangsu Hospital of Chinese Medicine (The Affiliated Hospital of Nanjing University of Chinese Medicine)
8	江苏省肿瘤医院（南京医科大学附属肿瘤医院，江苏省肿瘤防治研究所，江苏省红十字肿瘤医院）	Jiangsu Oncology Hospital (The Affiliated Tumor Hospital of Nanjing Medical University / Jiangsu Oncology Institute / Jiangsu Red Cross Tumor Hospital)
9	明基医院（南京医科大学附属明基医院）	BenQ Medical Center (BenQ Medical Center Affiliated to Nanjing Medical University)
10	南京国际（SOS）紧急救援诊所	Nanjing International (SOS) Emergency Clinic
11	南京红十字血液中心	Nanjing Red Cross Blood Center
12	南京江北医院	Nanjing Jiangbei Hospital
13	南京江宁莱佛士诊所	Raffles Medical Nanjing Jiangning Clinic
14	南京脑科医院（南京医科大学附属脑科医院）	Nanjing Brain Hospital (The Brain Hospital Affiliated to Nanjing Medical University)
15	南京市第二医院	Nanjing No. 2 Hospital
16	南京市第一医院（南京医科大学附属南京医院，南京市心血管病医院，中国药科大学南京市第一医院）	Nanjing No. 1 Hospital (Nanjing Hospital Affiliated to Nanjing Medical University / Nanjing Cardiovascular Hospital / CPU Nanjing No.1 Hospital)
17	南京市第一医院河西分院	Hexi Branch, Nanjing No.1 Hospital

续表

序号	中文	英文
18	南京市儿童医院（南京医科大学附属儿童医院，江苏省红十字儿童医院）	Nanjing Children's Hospital (The Children's Hospital Affiliated to Nanjing Medical University / Jiangsu Red Cross Children's Hospital)
19	南京市妇幼保健院（南京医科大学附属妇产医院）	Nanjing Women and Children's Health Hospital (The Women's Hospital Affiliated to Nanjing Medical University)
20	南京市高淳人民医院（江苏大学附属高淳医院）	Nanjing Gaochun People's Hospital (Gaochun Hospital Affiliated to Jiangsu University)
21	南京市红十字会	Red Cross Society of China (Nanjing Branch)
22	南京市急救中心	Nanjing Emergency Medical Center
23	南京市江宁区中医医院	Nanjing Jiangning District TCM Hospital
24	南京市江宁医院（南京医科大学附属江宁医院）	Nanjing Jiangning Hospital (Jiangning Hospital Affiliated to Nanjing Medical University)
25	南京市口腔医院（南京大学医学院附属口腔医院）	Nanjing Stomatological Hospital (The Stomatology Hospital Affiliated to the Medical School of Nanjing University)
26	南京市溧水区人民医院（东南大学附属中大医院溧水分院）	Nanjing Lishui District People's Hospital (Lishui Branch of Zhongda Hospital of Southeast University)
27	南京市溧水区中医医院［江苏省中西医结合医院（南部院区）］	Nanjing Lishui District TCM Hospital (Southern Branch, Jiangsu Hospital of Integrated Traditional Chinese and Western Medicine)
28	南京市六合区人民医院（扬州大学医学院附属六合医院）	Nanjing Luhe District People's Hospital (Luhe Hospital Affiliated to the Medical School of Yangzhou University)
29	南京市浦口区中医医院（南京市中医院浦口分院）	Nanjing Pukou District TCM Hospital (Pukou Branch, Nanjing TCM Hospital)
30	南京市中西医结合医院（南京中医药大学附属医院）	Nanjing Hospital of Integrated Traditional Chinese and Western Medicine (The Affiliated Hospital of Nanjing University of Chinese Medicine)

续表

序号	中文	英文
31	南京市中心医院	Nanjing Central Hospital
32	南京市中医院	Nanjing Hospital of Chinese Medicine
33	南京市中医院（南京中医药大学附属南京中医院，南京市体育医院）	Nanjing Hospital of Chinese Medicine (Nanjing Hospital of Chinese Medicine Affiliated to Nanjing University of Chinese Medicine / Nanjing Sports Hospital)
34	南京同仁医院（东南大学医学院附属医院）	Nanjing Tongren Hospital (The Affiliated Hospital of the Medical School of Southeast University)
35	南京医科大学第二附属医院（南京医科大学第二临床医学院，江苏省第二红十字医院）	No. 2 Affiliated Hospital of Nanjing Medical University (No. 2 Clinical Medicine School of Nanjing Medical University / Jiangsu No. 2 Red Cross Hospital)
36	南京医科大学第四附属医院	No. 4 Affiliated Hospital of Nanjing Medical University
37	南京医科大学附属逸夫医院	Sir Run Run Shaw Hospital Affiliated to Nanjing Medical University
38	南京医科大学口腔医学院（南京医科大学附属口腔医院，江苏省口腔医院）	Stomatology School of Nanjing Medical University (The Stomatology Hospital Affiliated to Nanjing Medical University / Jiangsu Stomatology Hospital)
39	南京医科大学眼科医院（江苏省红十字眼科医院）	Eye Hospital of Nanjing Medical University (Jiangsu Red Cross Eye Hospital)
40	南京医科大学友谊整形外科医院	Friendship Plastic Surgery Hospital of Nanjing Medical University
41	南京医师协会	Nanjing Medical Doctor Association
42	南京医学会	Nanjing Medical Association
43	南京紫金医院	Nanjing Zijin Hospital

续表

序号	中文	英文
44	泰康仙林鼓楼医院	Taikang Xianlin Drum Tower Hospital
45	中国医学科学院皮肤病医院	Dermatology Hospital of Chinese Academy of Medical Sciences

8. 医疗警示指示说明信息

序号	中文	英文
1	____ 型血液告急	Type ____ Blood in an Emergency!
2	爱国卫生监督	Patriotic Health Inspection
3	病员须知	Patient Guide
4	当心射线	CAUTION // Radiation
5	更年期保健	Menopause Health Care
6	患者入口	Patients Entrance
7	患者止步	Staff Only
8	急诊须知	Emergency Patient Guide
9	健康体检；常规体检	Health Check-Up
10	进入实验区，请穿好工作服	Lab Area // Workwear Required

续表

序号	中文	英文
11	剧毒物品	Toxic Materials
12	口腔修复	Prosthodontics
13	口腔预防	Preventive Dentistry
14	口腔正畸	Orthodontics Clinic
15	口腔种植	Oral Implantology
16	门诊须知	Outpatient Guide
17	免疫预防接种	Vaccination and Immunization
18	男宾止步	Women Only
19	请勿谈论病人隐私	Please Respect the Privacy of Our Patients
20	请在诊室外候诊	Please Wait Outside the Consulting Room
21	取报告须知	Lab Report Collection Guide
22	人工牙齿种植	Dental Implantology
23	锐器！请注意	CAUTION // Sharp Objects
24	生物安全	Biosafety
25	生物危险，请勿入内	Biohazard // No Admittance
26	探视入口	Visitors Entrance

续表

序号	中文	英文
27	探视时间	Visiting Hours
28	探视须知	Visitors' Guide
29	危机干预	Crisis Intervention
30	无偿献血	Voluntary Blood Donation
31	献血体检	Blood Donor Health Check
32	心理咨询	Psychological Counseling
33	医疗急救通道	Emergency Access
34	医学美容	Medical Cosmetology
35	易燃物品	Flammable Materials
36	营养咨询	Nutrition Counseling
37	远程会诊	Telemedicine
38	住院须知	Admission Guide

七、政务服务

Part 7 Government services

1. 范围

本部分规定了南京市政务服务领域英文译写的相关术语和定义、译写要求和方法等。

本部分适用于南京市政务服务信息的英文译写。

2. 规范性引用文件

应用本部分内容需参考如下文件。如文件注明日期，则仅注日期的版本适用于本文件。如文件未注日期，则其最新版本（包括所有的修改单）适用于本部分。

汉语拼音方案（1958 年中华人民共和国第一届全国人民代表大会第五次会议审议通过）

GB 17733 地名 标志

GB/T 10001（所有部分）标志用公共信息图形符号

GB/T 16159 汉语拼音正词法基本规则

GB/T 30240.1—2013 公共服务领域英文译写规范(第1部分: 通则)

3. 术语和定义

下列术语和定义适用于本部分。

政务服务场所 government service venues

政府各级行政部门根据法律法规或审批权限，对社会团体、企事业单位和个人办理相关业务的地点。

4. 译写要求

4.1　政务服务领域公共场所中文标识在 GB/T 10001.1 中已经规定了相应的图形符号时，应首先按照标准的规定使用公共信息图形符号。使用国际通用标识符号或图标的，可不提供英文译写。

4.2　政务服务领域公共场所中文标识采用英文译写时，英文单词的大小写应符合本指南第 1 部分的规定；采用汉语拼音标注时，拼写应符合 GB/T 16159 的规定。

5. 译写方法

5.1　政务服务领域的英文译写应简单清晰，尽可能少用冠词、介词、形容词。

5.2　机构的翻译一般按“属地（或上级机构）+ 服务内容 + 机构名”的公式，如：“秦淮区投资建设代办服务中心”Qinhuai District Investment and Construction Agency Service Center。

5.3　政务服务内容的译写可以考虑从动宾结构出发，用宾语词修饰动词的抽象名词。如：服务内容是“认定教师资格”，即 authenticate the teacher certificate，动词的抽象名词是 authentification，所以翻译成 Teacher Certificate Authentification。同样，“进出口企业备案”中的动词的抽象名词是“备案”，即 registration，所以可翻译成 Import and Export Enterprise Registration。

5.4　政务服务信息的英文译写应符合 GB/T 30240.1 的规定。采用英文直接译写时，应符合国际通用惯例。

政务服务英文译法示例

注：1. 以下词条在各自二级目录下按照汉语拼音字母的顺序排列（若词条以阿拉伯数字或英文字母开头，则置于表首。数字先排，从小到大；字母后排，按照字母表顺序）。

2. “〔 〕”中的内容是对英文译法的解释说明。“（ ）”及其所包含的内容如果是词条的组成部分应保留，如果是词条的缩写、简称或其它同义词语则可根据实际情况选择使用。

3. “／”表示“和”或者“或”，如果是词条的组成部分应保留，如果表示选择关系则根据情况选择使用。“//”表示换行。

1. 政务服务机构名称

序号	中文	英文
1	____ 村便民服务站	____ Village Public Service Station
2	____ 街道便民服务中心	____ Subdistrict Public Service Center
3	____ 区公共法律服务中心	____ District Public Legal Service Center
4	____ 区政务服务中心公安出入境分中心	Public Security Bureau Exit-Entry Management Sub-Center, ____ District Government Service Center
5	____ 区政务服务中心婚姻登记分中心	Marriage Registration Sub-Center, ____ District Government Service Center
6	____ 区政务服务中心经济开发区分中心	Economic Development Zone Sub-Center, ____ District Government Service Center
7	____ 区政务服务中心就业管理分中心	Employment Management Sub-Center, ____ District Government Service Center

续表

序号	中文	英文
8	____ 区政务服务中心社保管理分中心	Social Security Management Sub-Center, ____ District Government Service Center
9	____ 区政务服务中心社保医保分中心	Social Security and Medical Insurance Sub-Center, ____ District Government Service Center
10	____ 区政务服务中心税务分中心	Taxation Administration Sub-Center, ____ District Government Service Center
11	国家税务总局南京市 ____ 区税务局分中心	Nanjing ____ District Taxation Bureau Sub-Center, State Taxation Administration
12	惠企综合服务平台	Comprehensive Business Service Platform
13	南京市 ____ 区 12345 热线中心	Nanjing ____ District 12345 Hotline Center
14	南京市 ____ 区服务中心	Nanjing ____ District Service Center
15	南京市 ____ 区公安分局行政服务中心	Administrative Service Center, ____ District Branch of Nanjing Municipal Public Security Bureau
16	南京市 ____ 区行政审批局	Nanjing ____ District Administrative Approval Bureau
17	南京市 ____ 区市民中心	Nanjing ____ District Civic Center
18	南京市 ____ 区投资建设代办服务中心	Nanjing ____ District Investment and Construction Agency Service Center
19	南京市 ____ 区政务服务管理办公室	Nanjing ____ District Government Service Administration Office
20	南京市 ____ 区政务服务中心	Nanjing ____ District Government Service Center
21	南京市 12345 热线中心	Nanjing 12345 Hotline Center
22	南京市公共资源交易中心	Nanjing Public Resource Trading Center

续表

序号	中文	英文
23	南京市公共资源交易中心 ____ 分中心	____ Sub-Center, Nanjing Public Resource Trading Center
24	南京市海外人才企业服务中心	Nanjing Service Center for Work and Entrepreneurship by Overseas Specialists
25	南京市投资建设代办服务中心	Nanjing Investment and Construction Agency Service Center
26	南京市政务服务中心	Nanjing Municipal Government Service Center
27	南京市政务服务中心房产交易与不动产登记分中心 ____ 办理点	____ Office, Real Estate Transaction and Registration Sub-Center, Nanjing Municipal Government Service Center
28	南京市政务服务中心公安车辆管理分中心	Public Security Bureau Vehicle Management Sub-Center, Nanjing Municipal Government Service Center
29	南京市政务服务中心公安出入境管理分中心	Public Security Bureau Exit-Entry Management Sub-Center, Nanjing Municipal Government Service Center
30	南京市政务服务中心社保分中心	Social Security Sub-Center, Nanjing Municipal Government Service Center
31	南京市政务服务中心医保分中心	Medical Insurance Sub-Center, Nanjing Municipal Government Service Center

2. 政务服务业务名称

序号	中文	英文
1	不见面审批	No Meeting Approval
2	长三角“一网通办”	Yangtze River Delta One-Visit Online Services
3	城乡居民养老保险	Urban-Rural Resident Old-Age Insurance

续表

序号	中文	英文
4	代办服务	Agency Services
5	法律援助	Legal Aid
6	防雷装置竣工验收	Lightning Protection Device Installation Acceptance Check
7	防雷装置设计审核	Lightning Protection Device Installation Design Examination
8	放射诊疗许可业务	Radiation Therapy Permit
9	服务热线	Service Hotline
10	港澳台居住证	Residence Permit for People from Hong Kong, Macao and Taiwan
11	工程建设业务	Construction Project Services
12	工伤医疗	Work-Related Injury Medical Care Services
13	公共场所卫生许可业务	Public Hygiene Permit
14	公证服务	Notary Services
15	公租房（业务）	Public Rental Housing
16	海外人才引进绿色通道	Green Channel for Overseas Specialists
17	监督热线	Supervision Hotline
18	建设工程规划许可业务	Construction & Engineering Planning Permit
19	教师资格认定	Teacher Certificate Authentification

续表

序号	中文	英文
20	进出口企业备案	Import and Export Enterprise Registration
21	居住证办理、登记、续期	Residence Permit Application, Registration and Renewal
22	跨城通办	Inter-City Services
23	跨省通办	Inter-Provincial Services
24	跨域通办	Inter-Regional Services
25	老年人绿色通道	Green Channel for Elderly Residents
26	免费复印服务	Free Photocopying Services
27	民生服务	Service for People's Wellbeing
28	民政事务服务	Civil Affairs Services
29	民族宗教类业务	Ethnic & Religious Affairs Services
30	排污许可类业务	Pollution Discharge Permit
31	企业投资项目备案	Enterprise Investment Project Registration
32	人才服务	Services to Specialists
33	人才引进	Specialists Recruitment
34	社会救助	Social Aid
35	生育及医疗保险	Maternity and Medical Insurance

续表

序号	中文	英文
36	失业保险	Unemployment Insurance
37	失业补助金	Unemployment Subsidies
38	施工图集中审查	Review of Construction Drawings
39	施工许可类业务	Construction Permit
40	市政规划业务	Municipal Urban Planning
41	事业单位法人登记业务	Public Institution Legal Person Registration
42	首问责任制	First Handler Responsibility System
43	数字证书	Digital Certificate
44	统一社会信用代码	Unified Social Credit Code
45	统一身份认证	Unified Identity Authentication
46	网上登记受理	Online Registration
47	危险化学品经营许可业务	Hazardous Chemicals Use Permit
48	一次性告知制	One-Visit Notification System
49	医疗保障服务	Medical Security Services
50	医疗机构执业许可业务	Medical Institution Operation Permit
51	医疗救助	Medical Aid

续表

序号	中文	英文
52	志愿者服务岗	Volunteer Service Post

3. 政务服务窗口名称

序号	中文	英文
1	“放管服”改革综合专窗	Administration Streamlining Reform Services
2	不动产登记资料查询与挂失	Document Inquiry & Loss Reporting for Real Estate Registration
3	不动产交易登记一件事	One-Visit for Real Estate Transaction and Registration
4	测绘和验线综合服务	Surveying and Mapping & Layout Check Services
5	出入境业务办理	Exit and Entry
6	发改业务综合受理	Development and Reform Projects Services
7	法人账号业务	Legal Person Account
8	个人征信	Personal Credit Affairs
9	工程建设并联审批咨询	Engineering Construction Joint Approval Consultation
10	工信业务综合受理	Industry and Information Technology Services
11	公共自行车综合业务	Shared Bike Management

续表

序号	中文	英文
12	规划业务综合受理	Planning Services
13	互联网 + 政务服务	Internet + Government Services
14	环境卫生业务综合办理	Public Sanitation Management
15	建设工程规划许可证	Construction & Engineering Planning Permit
16	建设工程竣工验收备案	Construction & Engineering Project Acceptance Recordation
17	建筑垃圾工程业务综合办理	Construction Waste Engineering Management
18	建筑业企业资质核准相关	Construction Enterprise Accreditation
19	交通业务综合受理（发证、咨询）	Transportation Services (Certificate Issuance and Consultation)
20	绿化园林综合业务受理	Forestry and Parks Services
21	农业农村业务综合受理	Agriculture and Rural Affairs
22	企业服务综合窗口	Enterprise Integrated Service
23	企业征信	Enterprise Credit
24	商务业务综合受理	Commerce Services
25	社会组织业务	Social Organizations Services
26	生态环境业务综合受理	Ecological & Environmental Matters Services
27	食品及医疗器械	Food and Medical Equipment

续表

序号	中文	英文
28	市容市貌业务综合办理	Cityscape Management Services
29	市政设施建设类审批	Urban Facilities Construction Review and Approval
30	水务业务综合受理	Water Management Services
31	司法业务综合受理	Judicial Affairs
32	通办综合服务窗口；综合受理窗口	One-Visit Service Counter 或 Comprehensive Services
33	通信行业管理业务	Telecommunications Industry Management Services
34	投资建设代办服务	Investment and Construction Agency Services
35	外国高端人才确认函	Letter of Verification for High-Level International Specialists
36	外国人来华工作许可	Non-Chinese National Work Permit
37	外国人来华申请	Visa Application
38	卫生健康业务综合受理	Healthcare and Sanitation Services
39	文化旅游业务综合受理	Culture and Tourism Services
40	文物考古业务综合受理	Cultural Relics and Archaeology Services
41	问询、导引	Inquiry
42	消防事项综合服务	Fire Prevention Services
43	信用查询事项	Credit Inquiry

续表

序号	中文	英文
44	一站式收费	One-Visit Payment
45	营业执照发放	Business License Issuance
46	应急管理业务综合受理	Emergency Management
47	优秀外籍高校毕业生来宁就业创业办理工作许可	Work and Startup Permit for Outstanding International University Graduates in Nanjing
48	政府投资城建项目立项审批	Government-Funded Urban Development Project Permit
49	主题综合服务专区 / 专窗	Integrated Services on Special Issues
50	自然资源业务综合受理	Natural Resources Application
51	综合收费	General Services to Enterprises General Payment
52	综合业务办理	General Services

八、组织机构、职务职称

Part 8 Institutional names, positions and professional titles

1. 范围

本部分规定了南京市组织机构、职务职称英文译写的相关术语和定义、译写要求和方法等。

本部分适用于南京市党政机关、企事业单位和人民团体等组织机构名称和职务职称用于对外交往和服务时的英文译写。

2. 规范性引用文件

应用本部分内容需参考如下文件。如文件注明日期，则仅注日期的版本适用于本文件。如文件未注日期，则其最新版本（包括所有的修改单）适用于本部分。

汉语拼音方案（1958 年中华人民共和国第一届全国人民代表大会第五次会议审议通过）

GB 17733 地名 标志

GB/T 10001（所有部分）标志用公共信息图形符号

GB/T 16159 汉语拼音正词法基本规则

GB/T 30240.1—2013 公共服务领域英文译写规范（第 1 部分：通则）

3. 术语和定义

下列术语和定义适用于本部分。

3.1 组织机构 institutional names

南京市党政机关、企事业单位和人民团体等组织机构的名称。

3.2 职务职称 positions and professional titles

职务指根据不同的职位类别设置的一系列职位的集合或统称。职称指区别专业技术或学术水平的等级称号。

4. 译写要求和方法

4.1 译写要求

4.1.1 “中国共产党”“中国人民政治协商会议”等在组织机构名称中出现时，经常使用缩写，“中国共产党”的英文缩写为CPC，“中国人民政治协商会议”的英文缩写为CPPCC，放在名称的最前面，如：“中国共产党南京市委员会”CPC Nanjing Municipal Committee。

4.1.2 南京市政府及下设部门、机构，通常译出限定词Municipal，如：“南京市人民政府”Nanjing Municipal People’s Government，“南京市财政局”Nanjing Municipal Finance Bureau。Municipal在不影响原释义的情况下也可略去，如：“南京市体育局”Nanjing Sports Bureau，“南京市玄武区教育局”Nanjing Xuanwu District Education Bureau。

4.1.3 组织机构名称中属性名单词较多且结构复杂，译写时应置于委员会、局和处等通名之后，如：“南京市城乡建设委员会”Nanjing Municipal Commission of Urban-Rural Development。如果属性名较短且结构简单，可置于通名之前，如：“南京市司法局”Nanjing Municipal Justice Bureau。

4.1.4 组织机构的从属关系应描述清晰完整，将下一级单位放在前面，上一级单位放在后面，中间用逗号或of隔开，如：“南京市江宁公安分局行政服务中心”Administrative Service Center, Jiangning District Branch of Nanjing Municipal Public Security Bureau。

4.1.5 译写时，一般不用定冠词，如：“南京市教育局”Nanjing Municipal Education Bureau。组织机构名称中有“中国共产党”“中国人民政治协商会议”等国家级固定名词时，须加上定冠词，如：“中共南京市委办公厅” General Office of Nanjing Municipal Committee of the Communist Party of China。

4.1.6 翻译组织机构名称时，优先参照上级同类机关的习惯译法。

4.2 组织机构名称

4.2.1 委员会可译作 Committee 或 Commission。党政机关作为集体领导组织的委员会，一般译作 Committee，如：“中国共产党南京市委员会”Nanjing Municipal Committee of the Communist Party of China 或 CPC Nanjing Municipal Committee，“南京市人大监察和司法委员会”Supervisory and Judicial Affairs Committee, Nanjing Municipal People's Congress。拥有一定行政管理权力的市级委员会，一般译作 Commission，如：“南京市发展和改革委员会”Nanjing Municipal Commission of Development and Reform，“中共南京市委政法委员会”Political and Legal Affairs Commission of Nanjing Municipal Committee of the Communist Party of China。人大、政协的工作委员会译作 ...Work Committee 或 ...Affairs Committee。如果使用 Affairs 说明其工作内容，work 应省略，如：“南京市人大常委会预算工作委员会”Budgetary Affairs Committee, the Standing Committee of Nanjing Municipal People's Congress。党的工作委员会（简称党工委）是各级党组织委员会派出的领导机构，译作 Working Committee，如：“仙林街道党工

委”CPC Xianlin Subdisctrict Working Committee。管理委员会译作 Administrative Committee，如：“南京江宁高新区管理委员会”Nanjing Jiangning Hi-Tech Industrial Development Zone Administrative Committee。

4.2.2 局一般译作 Bureau，具体行政级别或隶属关系应完整译出，如：“南京市科技局”Nanjing Municipal Bureau of Science and Techonology，“南京市玄武区商务局”Nanjing Xuanwu District Commerce Bureau。

4.2.3 处一般译作 Division，如：“行政处”Administrative Division。公共场所的“管理处”译作 Management Office，如：“市场管理处”Market Management Office。秘书处译作 Secretariat。

4.2.4 行政机构中履行执法职能的总队、大队、中队等一律译作 Unit，其级别自然体现在所属机构的行政级别，如：“南京市公安局治安总队”Public Order Unit of Nanjing Municipal Public Security Bureau。

4.2.5 协会译作 Association，联合会译作 Federation，学会译作 Association 或 Society。

4.2.6 非常设机构：领导小组译作 Leading Group；指挥部译作 Headquarters；联席会议译作 Joint Meeting；组委会译作 Organizing Committee；执委会译作 Executive Committee。

4.2.7 其他组织机构的译写应符合 GB/T 30240.1—2013 中第 5.2 条的各项要求。

4.3 行政区划限定成分

4.3.1 行政区划限定成分使用汉语拼音拼写，如：“六合区”Luhe District。

4.3.2 作为限定成分，行政区划名中的“市”“区”“县”“乡（镇）”“街道”等可省去不译，但在党政机关名称中应用英文译出，如：“高淳区教育局”Gaochun District Education Bureau。

4.3.3 区译作 District，如：“秦淮区”Qinhuai District。新区译作 New Area，如：“江北新区”Jiangbei New Area。街道译作 Subdistrict，如：“栖霞街道”Qixia Subdistrict。社区译作 Community，如：“石头城社区”Shitoucheng Community。村译作 Village，如：“兴隆村”Xinglong Village。

4.4 职务职称

4.4.1 各级党组织书记译作 Secretary，党委、人大、政府、政协等领导机关的秘书长译作 Secretariat Director。

4.4.2 主席译作 Chair 或 Chairperson（不分性别）。

4.4.3 委员会主任译作 Chair 或 Chairperson（不分性别）。主任（厅局级）译作 Director-General，主任（处级）译作 Director。

4.4.4 部长、局长（厅局级）译作 Director-General，局长（处级）译作 Director。

4.4.5 “副”用于党政机关领导职务时可选择使用 Vice 或 Deputy。Vice 一般用于表述 Mayor、Chair、President 的副职，如：“副市长”Vice Mayor，“副主席”Vice Chair，“副院长”Vice President。Deputy 一般用于 Secretary、Director 的副职，如：“副书记”Deputy Secretary，“副主任”Deputy Director。“常务副”职可译作 Executive Deputy 或 Executive Vice，如：“常务副市长”Executive Vice Mayor。Vice 或 Deputy 后不带连字符“-”。

4.4.6 “代”职通常译作 Acting，如：“代市长”Acting Mayor，“代区长”Acting District Mayor。

4.4.6　综合管理类公务员职级一般用“Level+罗马数字”表示，如：“一级巡视员”Level I Bureau Rank Official，“一级调研员”Level I Division Rank Official，“一级主任科员”Level I Principal Staff Member，“一级科员”Level I Staff Member。

4.2.7　其他职务职称的译写应符合GB/T 30240.1—2013的规定。

组织机构、职务职称英文译法示例

注：1. 组织机构名称参照党政机关相关文件的规范和惯例进行排序。

2. “〔 〕”中的内容是对英文译法的解释说明。“（ ）”及其所包含的内容如果是词条的组成部分应保留，如果是词条的缩写、简称或其它同义词语则可根据实际情况选择使用。

3. “/”表示“和”或者“或”，如果是词条的组成部分应保留，如果表示选择关系则根据情况选择使用。“//”表示换行。

1. 南京市市级组织机构名称

（1）中共南京市委相关组织机构名称

序号	中文	英文
1	中国共产党南京市委员会	Nanjing Municipal Committee of the Communist Party of China 或 CPC Nanjing Municipal Committee
2	中共南京市纪律检查委员会机关	Nanjing Discipline Inspection Committee of the Communist Party of China
3	中共南京市委办公厅	General Office of Nanjing Municipal Committee of the Communist Party of China
4	中共南京市委组织部	Organization Department of Nanjing Municipal Committee of the Communist Party of China
5	中共南京市委宣传部	Publicity Department of Nanjing Municipal Committee of the Communist Party of China
6	中共南京市委统一战线工作部	United Front Work Department of Nanjing Municipal Committee of the Communist Party of China
7	中共南京市委社会工作部	Society Work Department of Nanjing Municipal Committee of the Communist Party of China

续表

序号	中文	英文
8	中共南京市委政法委员会	Political and Legal Affairs Commission of Nanjing Municipal Committee of the Communist Party of China
9	中共南京市委研究室	Research Office of Nanjing Municipal Committee of the Communist Party of China
10	中共南京市委网络安全和信息化委员会办公室	Office of Cyberspace Affairs Commission of Nanjing Municipal Committee of the Communist Party of China
11	中共南京市委机构编制委员会办公室	Office of Organizational Setup Commission of Nanjing Municipal Committee of the Communist Party of China
12	中共南京市委金融委员会办公室	Office of Finance Commission of Nanjing Municipal Committee of the Communist Party of China
13	中共南京市委台湾工作办公室	Taiwan Work Office of Nanjing Municipal Committee of the Communist Party of China
14	中共南京市委市级机关工作委员会	Party and Government Offices Work Committee of Nanjing Municipal Committee of the Communist Party of China
15	中共南京市委巡察工作领导小组办公室	Office of the Inspection Leading Group of Nanjing Municipal Committee of the Communist Party of China
16	中共南京市委老干部局	Retired Officials Bureau of Nanjing Municipal Committee of the Communist Party of China
17	中共南京市委机要保密局	Bureau of Classified Documents Protection and Transmission of Nanjing Municipal Committee of the Communist Party of China

（2）南京市人大相关组织机构名称

序号	中文	英文
1	南京市人大常务委员会	The Standing Committee of Nanjing Municipal People's Congress

续表

序号	中文	英文
2	南京市人大常委会办公厅	General Office of the Standing Committee of Nanjing Municipal People's Congress
3	南京市人大监察和司法委员会	Supervisory and Judicial Affairs Committee, Nanjing Municipal People's Congress
4	南京市人大财政经济委员会	Financial and Economic Affairs Committee, Nanjing Municipal People's Congress
5	南京市人大法制委员会	Legislative Affairs Committee, Nanjing Municipal People's Congress
6	南京市人大社会建设委员会	Social Development Committee, Nanjing Municipal People's Congress
7	南京市人大常委会预算工作委员会	Budgetary Affairs Committee, the Standing Committee of Nanjing Municipal People's Congress
8	南京市人大常委会法制工作委员会	Legislative Affairs Committee, the Standing Committee of Nanjing Municipal People's Congress
9	南京市人大常委会农业和农村工作委员会	Agriculture and Rural Affairs Committee, the Standing Committee of Nanjing Municipal People's Congress
10	南京市人大常委会教育科学文化卫生委员会	Education, Science, Culture, and Public Health Committee, the Standing Committee of Nanjing Municipal People's Congress
11	南京市人大常委会环境资源城乡建设委员会	Environment, Resources, and Urban and Rural Construction Committee, the Standing Committee of Nanjing Municipal People's Congress
12	南京市人大常委会民族宗教侨务外事委员会	Ethnic, Religious, Overseas Chinese and Foreign Affairs Committee, the Standing Committee of Nanjing Municipal People's Congress
13	南京市人大常委会代表工作委员会	Deputy Affairs Committee, the Standing Committee of Nanjing Municipal People's Congress

（3）南京市政府相关组织机构名称

序号	中文	英文
1	南京市人民政府	Nanjing Municipal People's Government
2	南京市人民政府办公厅	General Office of Nanjing Municipal People's Government
3	南京市发展和改革委员会	Nanjing Municipal Commission of Development and Reform
4	南京市教育局	Nanjing Municipal Education Bureau
5	南京市科学技术局	Nanjing Municipal Bureau of Science and Technology
6	南京市工业和信息化局	Nanjing Municipal Bureau of Industry and Information Technology
7	南京市公安局	Nanjing Municipal Public Security Bureau
8	南京市民政局	Nanjing Municipal Civil Affairs Bureau
9	南京市司法局	Nanjing Municipal Justice Bureau
10	南京市财政局	Nanjing Municipal Finance Bureau
11	南京市人力资源和社会保障局	Nanjing Municipal Bureau of Human Resources and Social Security
12	南京市规划和自然资源局	Nanjing Municipal Bureau of Planning and Natural Resources
13	南京市生态环境局	Nanjing Municipal Bureau of Ecology and Environment
14	南京市城乡建设委员会	Nanjing Municipal Commission of Urban-Rural Development
15	南京市住房保障和房产局	Nanjing Municipal Bureau of Housing Security and Real Estate

续表

序号	中文	英文
16	南京市交通运输局	Nanjing Municipal Transport Bureau
17	南京市水务局	Nanjing Water Authority
18	南京市城市管理局	Nanjing Municipal Bureau of Urban Management
19	南京市绿化园林局	Nanjing Municipal Bureau of Forestry and Parks
20	南京市农业农村局	Nanjing Municipal Bureau of Agriculture and Rural Affairs
21	南京市商务局	Nanjing Municipal Commerce Bureau
22	南京市文化和旅游局	Nanjing Municipal Bureau of Culture and Tourism
23	南京市投资促进局	Nanjing Municipal Bureau of Investment Promotion
24	南京市卫生健康委员会	Nanjing Municipal Health Commission
25	南京市退役军人事务局	Nanjing Municipal Bureau of Veterans Affairs
26	南京市应急管理局	Nanjing Municipal Bureau of Emergency Management
27	南京市审计局	Nanjing Municipal Audit Bureau
28	南京市政府外事办公室	Foreign Affairs Office of Nanjing Municipal People's Government
29	南京市政府国有资产监督管理委员会	State-Owned Assets Supervision and Administration Commission of Nanjing Municipal People's Government
30	南京市政府研究室	Research Office of Nanjing Municipal People's Government

续表

序号	中文	英文
31	南京市数据局	Nanjing Municipal Bureau of Data Affairs
32	南京市市场监督管理局	Nanjing Municipal Bureau of Market Regulation Administration
33	南京市体育局	Nanjing Municipal Sports Bureau
34	南京市统计局	Nanjing Municipal Statistics Bureau
35	南京市医疗保障局	Nanjing Municipal Bureau of Medical Security
36	南京市信访局	Nanjing Municipal Bureau of Public Complaints and Proposals
37	南京市民族宗教事务局	Nanjing Municipal Bureau of Ethnic and Religious Affairs
38	南京市国防动员办公室	Nanjing Municipal Office of Defense Mobilization
39	南京市机关事务管理局	Nanjing Municipal Administration of Government Offices

（4）南京市政协相关组织机构名称

序号	中文	英文
1	中国人民政治协商会议南京市委员会	Nanjing Municipal Committee of the Chinese People’s Political Consultative Conference 或 CPPCC Nanjing Municipal Committee
2	南京市政协办公厅（研究室）	General Office (Research Office) of the CPPCC Nanjing Municipal Committee
3	南京市政协提案委员会	Proposal Committee of the CPPCC Nanjing Municipal Committee

续表

序号	中文	英文
4	南京市政协经济科技委员会	Economic, Scientific and Technological Affairs Committee of the CPPCC Nanjing Municipal Committee
5	南京市政协人口资源环境（城市建设）委员会	Population, Resources and Environment (Urban Construction) Committee of the CPPCC Nanjing Municipal Committee
6	南京市政协教卫体（文化文史）委员会	Education, Health and Sports (Culture and History) Committee of the CPPCC Nanjing Municipal Committee
7	南京市政协社会法制（民族宗教）委员会	Social and Legal (Ethnic and Religious) Affairs Committee of the CPPCC Nanjing Municipal Committee
8	南京市政协港澳台侨和外事委员会	Hong Kong, Macao, Taiwan, Overseas Chinese and Foreign Affairs Committee of the CPPCC Nanjing Municipal Committee
9	南京市政协委员工作委员会	Member Affairs Committee of the CPPCC Nanjing Municipal Committee
10	南京市政协农业和农村工作委员会	Agriculture and Rural Affairs Committee of the CPPCC Nanjing Municipal Committee

（5）南京市法院、检察院、海关相关组织机构名称

序号	中文	英文
1	南京市中级人民法院	Nanjing Intermediate People's Court
2	审判庭	Adjudication Division
3	立案庭	Case-Filing Division
4	刑事审判庭	Criminal Division

续表

序号	中文	英文
5	民事审判庭	Civil Division
6	经济审判庭	Economic Division
7	行政审判庭	Administrative Division
8	审判监督庭	Judicial Supervision Division
9	执行庭	Enforcement Division
10	南京市人民检察院	Nanjing People's Procuratorate
11	海关	Customs
12	口岸	Port of Entry
13	边防口岸	Border Checkpoint

（6）南京市群众团体相关组织机构名称

序号	中文	英文
1	南京市总工会	Nanjing Federation of Trade Unions
2	南京市妇女联合会	Nanjing Women's Federation
3	南京市 ____ 联合会	Nanjing ____ Federation

续表

序号	中文	英文
4	南京市 ____ 工会	Nanjing ____ Trade Union
5	南京市 ____ 协会	Nanjing ____ Association
6	南京市 ____ 学会	Nanjing ____ Society 或 Nanjing ____ Association
7	南京市 ____ 中心	Nanjing ____ Center

（7）南京市政府派出机构

序号	中文	英文
1	南京江北新区管理委员会	Nanjing Jiangbei New Area Administrative Committee
2	南京经济技术开发区管理委员会	Nanjing Economic and Technological Development Zone Administrative Committee
3	南京市仙林大学城管理委员会	Nanjing Xianlin University Town Administrative Committee

（8）南京市其他组织机构名称

序号	中文	英文
1	南京市地方志编纂委员会办公室	Office of Nanjing Municipal Committee for Local Chronicles Compilation
2	中国国际贸易促进委员会南京分会	China Council for the Promotion of International Trade Nanjing Sub-Council (CCPIT NANJING)

续表

序号	中文	英文
3	南京市供销合作总社	Nanjing Supply and Marketing Cooperatives

2. 南京市区级组织机构名称

（1）南京市辖区名称

序号	中文	英文
1	玄武区	Xuanwu District
2	秦淮区	Qinhuai District
3	建邺区	Jianye District
4	鼓楼区	Gulou District
5	栖霞区	Qixia District
6	雨花台区	Yuhuatai District
7	江宁区	Jiangning District
8	浦口区	Pukou District
9	六合区	Luhe District
10	溧水区	Lishui District
11	高淳区	Gaochun District

（2）区级党委及群团相关组织机构名称

序号	中文	英文
1	中共南京市 ____ 区委	Nanjing ____ District Committee of the Communist Party of China 或 CPC Nanjing ____ District Committee
2	中共南京市 ____ 区纪律检查委员会监察委员会机关	Office of Nanjing ____ District CPC Discipline Inspection and Government Supervision Commissions
3	____ 区委办	Office of Nanjing ____ District Committee of the Communist Party of China
4	____ 区委组织部	Organization Department of Nanjing ____ District Committee of the Communist Party of China
5	____ 区委宣传部	Publicity Department of Nanjing ____ District Committee of the Communist Party of China
6	____ 区委统战部	United Front Work Department of Nanjing ____ District Committee of the Communist Party of China
7	____ 区委社会工作部	Society Work Department of Nanjing ____ District Committee of the Communist Party of China
8	____ 区政法委	____ District Political and Legal Affairs Committee
9	____ 区委研究室	Research Office of Nanjing ____ District Committee of the Communist Party of China
10	____ 区委编办	Office of Organization Setup Commission of Nanjing ____ District Committee of the Communist Party of China
11	____ 区委区级机关工委	Party and Government Offices Work Committee of Nanjing ____ District Committee of the Communist Party of China
12	____ 区残联	____ District Disabled People's Federation
13	____ 区关心下一代工作委员会	____ District Care-for-the-Next-Generation Work Committee

续表

序号	中文	英文
14	____ 区委党校	Party School of Nanjing ____ District Committee of the Communist Party of China
15	____ 区总工会	____ District Federation of Trade Unions
16	共青团 ____ 区委	Nanjing ____ District Committee of the Communist Youth League of China
17	____ 区妇女联合会	____ District Women's Federation
18	____ 区红十字会	Red Cross Society of China, Nanjing ____ District Branch
19	____ 街道工作委员会	CPC ____ Subdistrict Working Committee

（3）区人大相关组织机构名称

序号	中文	英文
1	____ 区人大常委会	Standing Committee of Nanjing ____ District People's Congress
2	____ 区人大监察和司法委员会	Supervisory and Judicial Affairs Committee, Nanjing ____ District People's Congress
3	____ 区人大财政经济委员会	Financial and Economic Affairs Committee, Nanjing ____ District People's Congress
4	____ 区人大法制委员会	Legislative Affairs Committee, Nanjing ____ District People's Congress
5	____ 区人大社会建设委员会	Social Development Committee, Nanjing ____ District People's Congress
6	____ 区人大常委会办公室	Office of the Standing Committee of Nanjing ____ District People's Congress
7	____ 区人大常委会研究室	Research Office, the Standing Committee of Nanjing ____ District People's Congress

续表

序号	中文	英文
8	____ 区人大常委会预算工作委员会	Budgetary Affairs Committee, the Standing Committee of Nanjing ____ District People's Congress
9	____ 区人大常委会农业和农村工作委员会	Agriculture and Rural Affairs Committee, the Standing Committee of Nanjing ____ District People's Congress
10	____ 区人大常委会教育科学文化卫生委员会	Education, Science, Culture and Public Health Committee, the Standing Committee of Nanjing ____ District People's Congress
11	____ 区人大常委会环境资源与城市建设委员会	Environment, Resources, and Urban Construction Committee, the Standing Committee of Nanjing ____ District People's Congress
12	____ 区人大常委会民族宗教侨台事务委员会	Ethnic, Religious, Overseas Chinese and Taiwan Affairs Committee, the Standing Committee of Nanjing ____ District People's Congress
13	____ 区人大常委会人事代表联络委员会	Deputy Liaison Committee, the Standing Committee of Nanjing ____ District People's Congress

（4）区政府相关组织机构名称

序号	中文	英文
1	南京市 ____ 区人民政府	Nanjing ____ District People's Government
2	____ 区人民政府办公室（政府外事办、政府研究室）	Office of Nanjing ____ District People's Government (Foreign Affairs Office of Nanjing ____ District People's Government, Research Office of Nanjing ____ District People's Government)
3	____ 区发展和改革委员会（大数据管理中心）	____ District Commission of Development and Reform (Big Data Management Center)

续表

序号	中文	英文
4	____ 区公安分局	____ District Branch of Nanjing Municipal Public Security Bureau
5	____ 派出所	____ Police Station
6	____ 区教育局	____ District Education Bureau
7	____ 区科学技术局	____ District Bureau of Science and Technology
8	____ 区工业和信息化局	____ District Bureau of Industry and Information Technology
9	____ 区民政局	____ District Bureau of Civil Affairs
10	____ 区司法局	____ District Justice Bureau
11	____ 区财政局	____ District Finance Bureau
12	____ 区人力资源和社会保障局	____ District Bureau of Human Resources and Social Security
13	____ 区城乡建设局	____ District Bureau of Urban Rural Development
14	____ 区住房保障和房产局	____ District Bureau of Housing Security and Real Estate
15	____ 区交通运输局	____ District Transport Bureau
16	____ 区水务局	____ District Water Authority
17	____ 区城市管理局	____ District Bureau of Urban Management
18	____ 区商务局	____ District Commerce Bureau
19	____ 区文化和旅游局	____ District Bureau of Culture and Tourism

续表

序号	中文	英文
20	____ 区体育局	____ District Sports Bureau
21	____ 区投资促进局	____ District Bureau of Investment Promotion
22	____ 区卫生健康委员会	____ District Health Commission
23	____ 区退役军人事务局	____ District Bureau of Veteran Affairs
24	____ 区应急管理局	____ District Bureau of Emergency Management
25	____ 区审计局	____ District Audit Bureau
26	____ 区人民政府国有资产监督管理办公室	____ District Office of State-Owned Assets Supervision and Administration
27	____ 区行政审批局（政务服务管理办公室）	____ District Bureau of Administrative Examination and Approval (Government Service Management Office)
28	____ 区农业农村局	____ District Bureau of Agriculture and Rural Affairs
29	____ 区税务局	____ District Taxation Bureau
30	____ 区消防大队	____ District Fire Brigade
31	____ 区市场监督管理局	____ District Bureau of Market Regulation Administration
32	____ 区统计局	____ District Statistics Bureau
33	____ 区信访局	____ District Bureau of Public Complaints and Proposals
34	____ 区国防动员办公室	____ District National Defense Mobilization Office

续表

序号	中文	英文
35	____ 区地方金融管理局（区政府金融工作办公室）	____ District Bureau of Local Financial Regulation (____ District Financial Market Affairs Office)
36	____ 区生态环境局	____ District Bureau of Ecology and Environment
37	南京市规划和自然资源局 ____ 分局	____ Branch of Nanjing Municipal Bureau of Resource Planning and Natural Resources
38	南京市医疗保障局 ____ 分局	____ Branch of Nanjing Municipal Medical Security Bureau
39	____ 管理委员会	____ Administration Committee
40	____ 街道	____ Subdistrict
41	____ 街道办事处	____ Subdistrict Office

（5）区政协相关组织机构名称

序号	中文	英文
1	____ 区政协办公室	____ Office of the CPPCC Nanjing District Committee
2	____ 区政协委员联络办公室	Liaison Office of the CPPCC Nanjing ____ District Committee
3	____ 区政协提案工作委员会	Proposal Affairs Committee of the CPPCC Nanjing ____ District Committee
4	____ 区政协经济科技委员会	Economic, Scientific and Technological Affairs Committee of the CPPCC Nanjing ____ District Committee
5	____ 区政协港澳台侨和外事工作委员会	Hong Kong, Macao, Taiwan, Overseas Chinese and Foreign Affairs Committee of the CPPCC Nanjing ____ District Committee

续表

序号	中文	英文
6	____ 区政协城乡建设专门委员会	Urban-Rural Construction Committee of the CPPCC Nanjing ____ District Committee
7	____ 区政协教卫文体工作委员会	Education, Health, Culture and Sports Committee of the CPPCC Nanjing ____ District Committee
8	____ 区政协社会法制（民族宗教）委员会	Social and Legal (Ethnic and Religious) Affairs Committee of the CPPCC Nanjing ____ District Committee

（6）区级法院、检察院组织机构名称

序号	中文	英文
1	____ 区人民法院	____ District People's Court
2	____ 区人民检察院	____ District People's Procuratorate

3. 南京市市级相关职务通用名称

（1）中共南京市委职务通用名称

序号	中文	英文
1	南京市委书记	Secretary of Nanjing Municipal Committee of the Communist Party of China 或 Secretary of the CPC Nanjing Municipal Committee
2	南京市委副书记	Deputy Secretary of Nanjing Municipal Committee of the Communist Party of China

续表

序号	中文	英文
3	南京市委秘书长	Secretariat Director of Nanjing Municipal Committee of the Communist Party of China
4	南京市委常务委员会委员	Member of the Standing Committee of Nanjing Municipal Committee of the Communist Party of China
5	市委组织部部长	Director of Organization Department of Nanjing Municipal Committee of the Communist Party of China
6	市委宣传部部长	Director of Publicity Department of Nanjing Municipal Committee of the Communist Party of China
7	市委统战部部长	Director of United Front Work Department of Nanjing Municipal Committee of the Communist Party of China

（2）南京市人大常委会职务通用名称

序号	中文	英文
1	南京市人大常委会主任	Chair of the Standing Committee of Nanjing Municipal People's Congress
2	南京市人大常委会副主任	Vice Chair of the Standing Committee of Nanjing Municipal People's Congress
3	南京市人大常委会秘书长	Secretariat Director of the Standing Committee of Nanjing Municipal People's Congress
4	南京市人大常务委员会委员	Member of the Standing Committee of Nanjing Municipal People's Congress

（3）南京市政府职务通用名称

序号	中文	英文
1	南京市市长	Mayor of Nanjing
2	南京市常务副市长	Executive Vice Mayor of Nanjing
3	南京市副市长	Vice Mayor of Nanjing
4	南京市政府秘书长	Secretariat Director of Nanjing Municipal People's Government
5	南京市政府副秘书长	Deputy Secretariat Director of Nanjing Municipal People's Government

（4）南京市政协职务通用名称

序号	中文	英文
1	南京市政协主席	Chair of the CPPCC Nanjing Municipal Committee
2	南京市政协副主席	Vice Chair of the CPPCC Nanjing Municipal Committee
3	南京市政协秘书长	Secretariat Director of the CPPCC Nanjing Municipal Committee
4	南京市政协常务委员	Member of the Standing Committee of the CPPCC Nanjing Municipal Committee

（5）南京市中级人民法院职务通用名称

序号	中文	英文
1	院长	President
2	副院长	Vice President
3	审判委员会专职委员	Standing Member of the Adjudication Committee
4	审判长	Presiding Judge
5	法官（审判员）	Judge
6	法官助理	Judicial Assistant
7	书记员	Clerk
8	庭长	Court Judge
9	副庭长	Deputy Court Judge

（6）南京市人民检察院职务通用名称

序号	中文	英文
1	检察长	Chief Procurator
2	副检察长	Deputy Chief Procurator
3	检察委员会专职委员	Member of Procuratorial Committee

续表

序号	中文	英文
4	检察员	Procurator
5	助理检察员	Assistant Procurator

（7）南京市级机关部、委、办、局职务通用名称

序号	中文	英文
1	党组	CPC Group
2	党组书记	Secretary of the CPC Group
3	党组副书记	Deputy Secretary of the CPC Group
4	党组成员	Member of the CPC Group
5	办公厅主任	Director-General of General Office
6	办公厅副主任	Deputy Director-General of General Office
7	____委员会书记	Secretary of ____ Committee
8	____委员会副书记	Deputy Secretary of ____ Committee
9	____委员会主任	Chair of ____ Commissioon
10	____委员会副主任	Vice Chair of ____ Commissioon

续表

序号	中文	英文
11	____ 部长	Director-General of ____ Department
12	____ 副部长	Deputy Director-General of ____ Department
13	____ 办公室主任	Director of ____ Office
14	____ 办公室副主任	Deputy Director of ____ Office
15	____ 局长（司局级）	Director-General of ____ Bureau
16	____ 副局长（司局级）	Deputy Director-General of ____ Bureau
17	工会主席	Chair of the Trade Union
18	工会副主席	Vice Chair of the Trade Union
19	____ 处长	Division Director of ____ Division
20	____ 副处长	Deputy Division Director of ____ Division

4. 南京市区级相关职务通用名称

（1）区委职务通用名称

序号	中文	英文
1	____ 区委书记	Secretary of Nanjing ____ District Committee of the Communist Party of China 或 Secretary of the CPC Nanjing ____ District Committee

续表

序号	中文	英文
2	____ 区委副书记	Deputy Secretary of Nanjing ____ District Committee of the Communist Party of China
3	____ 区委常务委员会委员	Member of the Standing Committee of Nanjing ____ District Committee of the Communist Party of China
4	____ 区委办主任	Director of Office of Nanjing ____ District Committee of the Communist Party of China
5	____ 区委办副主任	Deputy Director of Office of Nanjing ____ District Committee of the Communist Party of China

（2）区人大常委会职务通用名称

序号	中文	英文
1	____ 区人大常委会主任	Chair of the Standing Committee of Nanjing ____ District People's Congress
2	____ 区人大常委会副主任	Vice Chair of the Standing Committee of Nanjing ____ District People's Congress

（3）区政府职务通用名称

序号	中文	英文
1	____ 区区长	District Mayor of Nanjing ____ District People's Government
2	____ 区常务副区长	Executive Deputy District Mayor of Nanjing ____ District People's Government
3	____ 区副区长	Deputy District Mayor of Nanjing ____ District People's Government

续表

序号	中文	英文
4	____ 区政府办主任	Director of Office of Nanjing ____ District People's Government
5	____ 区政府办副主任	Deputy Director of Office of Nanjing ____ District People's Government

（4）区政协职务通用名称

序号	中文	英文
1	____ 区政协主席	Chair of the CPPCC Nanjing ____ District Committee
2	____ 区政协副主席	Vice Chair of the CPPCC Nanjing ____ District Committee

（5）区级委、办、局职务通用名称

序号	中文	英文
1	____ 局长（处级）	Director of ____ Bureau
2	____ 副局长（处级）	Deputy Director of ____ Bureau
3	____ 街道工委书记	Secretary of the CPC Nanjing ____ Subdistrict Working Committee
4	____ 办事处主任	Director of ____ Office
5	____ 街道工委副书记	Deputy Secretary of the CPC Nanjing ____ Subdistrict Working Committee

续表

序号	中文	英文
6	____ 街道工委委员	Member of the CPC Nanjing ____ Subdistrict Working Committee
7	____ 科科长	Section Chief of ____ Section
8	____ 科副科长	Deputy Section Chief of ____ Section

5. 综合管理类公务员职级名称

序号	中文	英文
1	一级巡视员	Level I Bureau Rank Official
2	二级巡视员	Level II Bureau Rank Official
3	一级调研员	Level I Division Rank Official
4	二级调研员	Level II Division Rank Official
5	三级调研员	Level III Division Rank Official
6	四级调研员	Level IV Division Rank Official
7	一级主任科员	Level I Principal Staff Member
8	二级主任科员	Level II Principal Staff Member
9	三级主任科员	Level III Principal Staff Member

续表

序号	中文	英文
10	四级主任科员	Level IV Principal Staff Member
11	一级科员	Level I Staff Member
12	二级科员	Level II Staff Member

九、南京特色词汇

Part 9 Nanjing culture

1. 范围

本部分规定了南京市特色词汇英文译写的相关术语和定义、译写要求和方法等。

本部分适用于南京市特色词汇的英文译写。

2. 规范性引用文件

应用本部分内容需参考如下文件。如文件注明日期，则仅注日期的版本适用于本文件。如文件未注日期，则其最新版本（包括所有的修改单）适用于本部分。

汉语拼音方案（1958 年中华人民共和国第一届全国人民代表大会第五次会议审议通过）

GB 17733 地名 标志

GB/T 10001（所有部分）标志用公共信息图形符号

GB/T 16159 汉语拼音正词法基本规则

GB/T 30240.1—2013 公共服务领域英文译写规范(第1部分: 通则)

3. 术语和定义

下列术语和定义适用于本部分。

南京市特色词汇 Nanjing culture

南京市特色词汇指南京城市名片、文博场馆、南京美食、产业发展、旅游景区等方面的独特词汇或短语。这些词汇代表了南京的独特魅力和城市形象。

4. 译写要求

4.1　译写既要符合英语使用习惯，准确表达原意，有助于塑造文明城市形象，又要反映南京历史文化内涵和人文特色，有利于对外交流及国际传播。

4.2　译写应符合 GB/T 30240.1—2013 的规定。

5. 译写方法

5.1　译写时信息要完整准确。如："渡江胜利纪念馆"中的"渡江胜利"应译出，可以译作 The Memorial Hall of the Victory of Crossing the Yangtze River Campaign。

5.2　译写时可以补充必要的信息。如：南京"世界文学之都"的称号由联合国科教文组织认定，因此译作 UNESCO City of Literature。

5.3　地方美食的翻译，在解释介绍菜肴时可以说明所用的主料、配料和烹制的方法。如："鸭血粉丝汤"可以译作 Duck Blood and Glass Noodle Soup，在宣传南京特色餐饮文化时，也可使用通俗简洁、容易上口、便于传播的译法，如：Duck Blood Glass Noodle Soup。

5.4　翻译有关产业方向的词汇时，Industry 可以省略，如："人工智能产业" Artificial Intelligence 或 Artificial Intelligence Industry。

南京特色词汇英文译法示例

注：1. 以下词条在各自二级目录下按照汉语拼音字母的顺序排列（若词条以阿拉伯数字或英文字母开头，则置于表首。数字先排，从小到大；字母后排，按照字母表顺序）。

2. “〔 〕”中的内容是对英文译法的解释说明。“（ ）”及其所包含的内容如果是词条的组成部分应保留，如果是词条的缩写、简称或其它同义词语则可根据实际情况选择使用。

3. “/”表示“和”或者“或”，如果是词条的组成部分应保留，如果表示选择关系则根据情况选择使用。“//”表示换行。

1. 城市名片

序号	中文	英文
1	奥运城市	Olympic City
2	八卦洲	Bagua Island
3	长江大保护	Yangtze River Protection Initiative
4	长江濒危物种	Endangered Species of the Yangtze River
5	长江江豚	Yangtze Finless Porpoise
6	长江经济带	Yangtze River Economic Belt
7	长江经济带重要节点城市	Important City in the Yangtze River Economic Belt

续表

序号	中文	英文
8	长江三角洲区域一体化	Integrated Development of the Yangtze River Delta
9	长江湿地	Yangtze Wetlands
10	长三角群特大城市	Megacity in the Yangtze River Delta Metropolitan Area
11	国际和平城市	International Peace City
12	国际消费中心城市	International Consumption Center
13	国家创新型城市	National City of Innovation
14	国家科技体制综合改革试点城市	National Pilot City for Comprehensive Reform of Science and Technology Systems
15	国家历史文化名城	National-Level Historical and Cultural City
16	国家森林城市	National Forest City
17	国家生态园林城市	National Ecological Garden City
18	国家文化和旅游消费示范城市	National Demonstration City for Culture and Tourist Consumption
19	夹江	Jiajiang River
20	江心洲	Jiangxinzhou Island
21	科创金融改革试验区（国家级）	National-Level Pilot Financial Reform Zone for Scientific and Technological Innovation
22	六朝古都	Ancient Capital of Six Dynasties
23	南京都市圈	Nanjing Metropolitan Circle

续表

序号	中文	英文
24	南京长江江豚自然保护区	Nanjing Yangtze Finless Porpoise Nature Reserve
25	潜洲	Qianzhou Island
26	全球金融中心城市	A Global Financial Center
27	生态科技岛	Eco Hi-Tech Island
28	十朝都会	Metropolis of Ten Dynasties and Regimes
29	世界文学之都	UNESCO City of Literature
30	水源地	Water Source Area
31	天下文枢	Cultural Center of the World
32	“一带一路”交汇点重要枢纽城市	Important Hub City of the Belt and Road
33	中国软件名城	National Software City
34	中国营商环境标杆城市	Benchmark City for Business Environment in China

2. 产业发展

（1）指导产业

序号	中文	英文
1	半导体产业	Semi-Conductor Industry〔Industry 可省略〕
2	储能	Energy Storage Industry〔Industry 可省略〕
3	电子信息产业	Electronic Information Industry〔Industry 可省略〕
4	高端商务商贸	High-End Business and Trade
5	轨道交通	Rail Transportation
6	航空航天产业	Aerospace Industry〔Industry 可省略〕
7	基因与细胞	Genes and Cells
8	集成电路产业	Integrated Circuit Industry〔Industry 可省略〕
9	科技服务	Hi-Tech Services
10	绿色经济	Green Economy
11	平台经济	Platform Economy
12	氢能	Hydrogen Power Industry〔Industry 可省略〕
13	人工智能产业	Artificial Intelligence Industry〔Industry 可省略〕
14	软件和信息服务产业	Software and Information Services Industry〔Industry 可省略〕

续表

序号	中文	英文
15	生命健康	Life and Health
16	生物医药产业	Biomedical Industry
17	石化、钢铁	Petrochemical Industry, Iron and Steel Industry〔Industry 可省略〕
18	体育产业	Sports Industry〔Industry 可省略〕
19	未来网络	Future Network
20	文旅产业	Culture and Tourism Industry〔Industry 可省略〕
21	现代金融	Modern Finance
22	现代物流	Modern Logistics
23	新能源汽车	New Energy Vehicle Industry〔Industry 可省略〕
24	新型材料产业	New Materials Industry〔Industry 可省略〕
25	新型电力	New Power Industry〔Industry 可省略〕
26	元宇宙	Metaverse Industry〔Industry 可省略〕
27	智能电网	Smart Grid Industry〔Industry 可省略〕
28	智能制造产业	Smart Manufacturing Industry〔Industry 可省略〕
29	总部经济	Headquarters Economy

（2）科创园区

序号	中文	英文
1	河西新城	Hexi New Town
2	江北新区产业技术研创园	Jiangbei New Area Industrial Technology Research and Innovation Park
3	江宁经济技术开发区（国家级）	Jiangning National-Level Economic and Technological Development Zone
4	科技创新示范园区	Sci-Tech Innovation Demonstration Zone
5	南部新城	Southern New Town
6	南京经济技术开发区（国家级）	Nanjing National-Level Economic and Technological Development Zone
7	南京临空经济示范区（国家级）	Nanjing National-Level Airport Economic Demonstration Zone
8	农业高新技术产业示范区（国家级）	Nanjing National-Level Agricultural High-Tech Industrial Demonstration Zone
9	仙林大学城	Xianlin University Town
10	新加坡南京生态科技岛	Singapore Nanjing Eco Hi-Tech Island
11	中国（江苏）自由贸易试验区南京片区	China (Jiangsu) Pilot Free Trade Zone (Nanjing Area)
12	中国（南京）软件谷	China (Nanjing) Software Valley

3. 南京市旅游景区

序号	中文	英文
1	百家湖 1912 夜间聚集区	Baijiahu Lake 1912 Nightlife Area
2	夫子庙全国示范步行街	Confucius Temple National Demonstration Pedestrian Street
3	傅家边农业科技观光园	Fujiabian Agricultural Science and Technology Park
4	华昌龙之谷	Huachang Dragon Valley
5	江北新区滨江风光带	Jiangbei New Area Riverside Scenic Belt
6	江苏园博园	Jiangsu Garden Expo Park
7	金牛湖野生动物王国	Jinniu Lake Wild Animals Kingdom
8	老门东	Laomendong
9	溧水白马如意文化艺术中心（周园）	Lishui Baima Ruyi Cultural and Art Center (Zhouyuan Garden)
10	绿博园	Green Expo Garden
11	梅钢工业文化旅游区	Meishan Iron and Steel Industrial Cultural Tourist Area
12	幕燕五马渡夜公园	Muyan Wumadu Night Park
13	南京国防园	Nanjing National Defense Park
14	南京欢乐谷景区	Nanjing Happy Valley Scenic Area
15	南京市朝天宫景区	Nanjing Chaotian Palace Scenic Area

续表

序号	中文	英文
16	南京市大报恩寺遗址公园景区	Nanjing Grand Baoen Temple Heritage and Scenic Area
17	南京市方山风景区	Nanjing Fangshan Mountain Scenic Area
18	南京市夫子庙—秦淮风光带景区	Nanjing Confucius Temple – Qinhuai Scenic Area
19	南京市高淳国际慢城	Nanjing Gaochun International Cittaslow
20	南京市高淳老街历史文化景区	Nanjing Gaochun Old Street Historial and Cultural Area
21	南京市红山森林动物园	Nanjing Hongshan Forest Zoo
22	南京市金牛湖景区	Nanjing Jinniu Lake Scenic Area
23	南京市老山森林公园景区	Nanjing Laoshan Mountain Forest Park
24	南京市明文化村（阳山碑材）景区	Nanjing Ming Dynasty Culture Village (Yangshan Monument Stone Blocks) Scenic Area
25	南京市莫愁湖公园景区	Nanjing Mochou Lake Park
26	南京市幕燕滨江风貌区	Nanjing Muyan Riverside Scenic Area
27	南京市牛首山文化旅游区	Nanjing Niushou Mountain Cultural Tourist Area
28	南京市平山森林公园	Nanjing Pingshan Mountain Forest Park
29	南京市栖霞山风景区	Nanjing Qixia Mountain Scenic Area
30	南京市石头城遗址公园	Nanjing Stone City Historical Site Park

续表

序号	中文	英文
31	南京市天生桥景区	Nanjing Tianshengqiao Scenic Area
32	南京市无想山景区	Nanjing Wuxiang Mountain Scenic Area
33	南京市玄武湖景区	Nanjing Xuanwu Lake Scenic Area
34	南京市游子山休闲旅游区	Nanjing Youzi Mountain Leisure Park
35	南京市雨花台风景区	Nanjing Yuhuatai Scenic Area
36	南京市阅江楼景区	Nanjing Yuejiang Tower Scenic Area
37	南京市珍珠泉风景区	Nanjing Pearl Spring Scenic Area
38	南京市钟山风景名胜区	Nanjing Zhongshan Mountain Scenic Area
39	南京眼旅游区	Nanjing Eye Tourist Spot
40	南京长江路文化和旅游集聚区	Nanjing Changjiang Road Cultural and Tourist Neighborhood
41	南艺后街·鼓楼水岸艺术街区	NUA Backstreet – Drum Tower Waterfront Art Block
42	清凉山公园	Qingliang Mountain Park
43	汤山紫清湖旅游区	Tangshan Mountain Ziqing Lake Tourist Resort
44	无想水镇	Wuxiang Water Town
45	熙南里历史文化休闲街区	Xinanli Historical and Cultural Block
46	新街口夜间文化和旅游消费集聚区	Xinjiekou Nightlife and Tourist Area

续表

序号	中文	英文
47	银杏里文化艺术街区	Yinxingli Cultural and Art Block
48	鱼嘴湿地公园灯塔	Yuzui Wetland Park Lighthouse
49	云幽谷旅游区	Yunyou Valley Tourist Attraction
50	中山陵园风景区	Dr. Sun Yat-sen's Mausoleum Scenic Area

4. 南京市文博场馆

序号	中文	英文
1	渡江胜利纪念馆	The Memorial Hall of the Victory of Crossing the Yangtze River Campaign
2	江宁织造博物馆	Jiangning Imperial Silk Manufacturing Museum
3	江苏大剧院	Jiangsu Center for the Performing Arts
4	金陵图书馆	Jinling Library
5	六朝博物馆	The Oriental Metropolitan Museum (Museum of Six Dynasties)
6	南京奥林匹克博物馆	Nanjing Olympic Museum
7	明孝陵博物馆	Ming Tomb Museum
8	南京保利大剧院	Nanjing Poly Grand Theater

续表

序号	中文	英文
9	南京博物院	Nanjing Museum
10	南京城墙博物馆	Nanjing City Wall Museum
11	南京地质博物馆	Nanjing Geological Museum
12	南京古生物博物馆	Nanjing Museum of Paleontology
13	南京静海寺纪念馆	Nanjing Jinghai Temple Memorial Hall
14	南京抗日航空烈士纪念馆	Nanjing Anti-Japanese Aviation Martyrs Memorial Hall (Nanjing Memorial Hall for Aviation Martyrs in the War of Resistance Against Japanese Aggression)
15	南京科技馆	Nanjing Science & Technology Museum
16	南京美术馆	Nanjing Art Museum
17	南京市博物馆（朝天宫）	Nanjing Municipal Museum (Chaotian Palace)
18	南京市民俗博物馆	Nanjing Folklore Museum
19	南京市现代陶瓷博物馆	Nanjing Modern Ceramics Museum
20	南京“世界文学客厅”	Nanjing “World Literature Salon”
21	南京太阳宫剧场	Nanjing Sun Palace Theater
22	南京图书馆	Nanjing Library
23	南京云锦博物馆	Nanjing Yunjin Brocade Museum

续表

序号	中文	英文
24	南京中国近代史遗址博物馆（总统府景区）	Nanjing Museum of Modern Chinese Historical Sites (Presidential Palace Scenic Area)
25	南京紫金山昆虫博物馆	Nanjing Purple Mountain Insect Museum
26	侵华日军南京大屠杀遇难同胞纪念馆	The Memorial Hall of the Victims of the Nanjing Massacre by Japanese Invaders
27	太平天国历史博物馆（瞻园）	Museum of the History of Taiping Heavenly Kingdom (Zhanyuan Garden)
28	雨花台烈士纪念馆	Yuhuatai Martyrs Memorial Hall
29	中国共产党代表团梅园新村纪念馆	Meiyuan Xincun Memorial Hall of the Delegation of the Communist Party of China
30	中国科举博物馆	China Imperial Civil Service Examination Museum
31	中国科学院紫金山天文台	Purple Mountain Observatory, Chinese Academy of Sciences

5. 南京美食

序号	中文	英文
1	板鸭	Nanjing Dried Salted Duck
2	炒菊花脑	Stir-Fried Chrysanthemum Leaves
3	炒空心菜	Stir-Fried Water Spinach
4	炒芦蒿	Stir-Fried Mugwort

续表

序号	中文	英文
5	炒荠菜	Stir-Fried Shepherd's Purse
6	炒丝瓜	Stir-Fried Towel Gourd
7	炒茼蒿	Stir-Fried Crown Daisy
8	炒苋菜	Stir-Fried Chinese Amaranth
9	赤豆元宵	Rice Balls With Lotus Seeds and Red Beans
10	东山老鹅	Dongshan Braised Goose
11	豆腐脑	Tofu Jelly
12	固城湖大闸蟹	Gucheng Lake Crabs
13	回卤干	Spiced Dried Bean Curd
14	金陵臭干	Jinling Style Fermented Bean Curd
15	金陵烤鸭	Jinling Roast Duck
16	金陵鸭宴	Jinling Duck Feast
17	金陵盐水鸭	Jinling Salted Duck
18	六合头道菜	Luhe Casserole
19	麻油素干丝	Shredded Dried Bean Curd in Sesame Oil
20	梅花糕	Plum Rice Cake

续表

序号	中文	英文
21	南京酱鸭头	Nanjing Stewed Duck Heads
22	南京香肚	Nanjing Sausage
23	南京小馄饨（汤）	Nanjing Mini-Wonton Soup
24	牛肉粉丝汤	Beef Noodle Soup
25	牛肉锅贴	Beef Potstickers
26	牛肉汤包	Beef Soup Buns
27	秦淮八绝	Qinhuai's Eight Signature Dishes
28	肉汁萝卜	Mooli Stewed in Gravy
29	什锦素菜包	Assorted Vegetable Buns
30	汤包	Soup Buns
31	糖醋排骨	Sweet and Sour Spare Ribs
32	糖粥藕	Sweet Lotus Root Porridge
33	五香蛋	Braised Eggs
34	蟹黄汤包	Crab Roe Soup Buns
35	鸭血粉丝汤	Duck Blood Glass Noodle Soup
36	鸭油酥烧饼	Duck Oil Pastry

续表

序号	中文	英文
37	雨花茶	Yuhua Tea 或 Rain Flower Tea
38	雨花石汤团	Yuhua Sweet Dumplings 或 Rain Flower Sweet Dumplings

《南京市公共服务领域英文译写指南》由南京市公共服务领域英文译写语库专家组负责起草，王守仁组长、丁言仁副组长审定，经南京市人民政府外事办公室组织实施并发布试行。

第一部分 通则：	王银泉 孙小春 陈 星
第二部分 道路交通：	刘 宝 汪璧辉 尹婵杰
第三部分 商业服务：	尹婵杰 王 祥 顾 静
第四部分 文化旅游：	刘 宝 孙小春
第五部分 教育体育：	陈尚坤 汪璧辉
第六部分 医疗卫生：	陈尚坤 甘 珏
第七部分 政务服务：	何山华 王 祥
第八部分 组织机构：	何山华 王 祥
第九部分 南京特色词汇：	孙小春 章 倜

欢迎关注市外办官方微信“南京外事港澳”公众号查阅本指南电子版，敬请留言提出宝贵意见！